motion

motion

American Sports Poems

Edited by Noah Blaustein

Foreword by John Edgar Wideman

University of Iowa Press Iowa City

University of Iowa Press, Iowa City 52242

Copyright © 2001 by the University of Iowa Press

All rights reserved

Printed in the United States of America

Design by Richard Hendel

http://www.uiowa.edu/~uipress

The publication of this book was generously supported by the
University of Iowa Foundation.

Grants were provided by the English department at University of
Massachusetts-Amherst, Stephen Clingman, chair.

Printed on acid-free paper

Library of Congress Cataloging-in-Publication Data
Motion: American sports poems / edited by Noah Blaustein.

      p.   cm.

   Includes index.

   ISBN 0-87745-754-9 (cloth), ISBN 0-87745-755-7 (pbk.)

   1. Sports—Poetry. 2. American Poetry. I. Blaustein, Noah, 1969–.

PS595.S78 M68 2001

811.008'0355–dc21   00-050938

01 02 03 04 05 C 5 4 3 2 1

01 02 03 04 05 P 5 4 3 2 1

For J.H.B. & J.A.B.

Contents

Foreword

Noah,

I like the idea of a book of poems about sports. I like the idea of think-
ing about the idea. Where to begin. What to include. What waits to be
discovered. Aren't there ancient odes celebrating the deeds of Greek ath-
letes? Do African praise songs recall legendary wrestlers, runners, danc-
ers? Does every language possess a corpus of poetry dedicated to sport?
Will your collection contain translations? Clearly, my curiosity is piqued,
and in lots of ways I'd enjoy doing what you're doing.

One reason I like the idea of a sports poem book is that sport, the
commodified, packaged, grotesquely overhyped and overmanaged con-
temporary manifestations of sport as entertainment, as frills for the vast,
vacant spaces of media, is pretty depressing. Sport as spectacle, as a ve-
hicle designed to make money by bringing together a minuscule cadre of
highly skilled doers with a mass audience of passive watchers feels inher-
ently suspect, rife with all sorts of possibilities/opportunities for manipu-
lation, exploitation, alienation, divisiveness, and isolation detrimental to
both watcher and watched. I'm already sidelined by too much else in
contemporary culture. Why must sport be stolen also? I need the sanctity,
the joy and power of my body rewarding sweaty, determined effort. Es-
pecially so given the immense scale and complexity of a world in which
machines are supposed to be making my life easier but in fact shrink the
significance of what's individual and personal, a world offering choices —
blue, pink, green, or yellow toilet paper — while it deprives me of the one
choice that actually matters: whether or not I want to accept the version
of reality prescribed by the assumptions generating the multiple choices.
Assumptions, for instance, about the use of trees, the quality of air trees
help to monitor, the power and ethics of corporations that control the
array of products consumers can choose from, and finally the bottomline
assumption that capitalism is good because it produces profit, while the
profit motive somehow supplies capitalism with a built-in conscience that
serves the interests of the majority, who possess little or no capital.

If religion is the opiate of the people, sport today is the people's crack.

Cheap, hot, addictive, immediate, sport provides a reductive mirror for life. Tells me the only thing that counts is being number one. And it doesn't matter how you get there. Media coverage of sports casts a net of simplistic metaphors into every corner of society. Inflated, breathless, violent, reductive bombast transforms everything from business deals to raising children into the *mano a mano*, confrontational terms of slam dunks, in-your-face, sacks, knockouts, winners and losers. Sport becomes the perfect reflection, a role model for our culture's selfish, unthinking, predatory drive toward monopoly, conformity, class stratification, toward self-aggrandizement, material accumulation, and conspicuous consumption.

Poets will provide an alternative view of sports, won't they? Won't poets conjure sports away from the dreariness of scores, inflated egos, profits, scandal, into realms of creative self-expression, spirit, play for the sake of play? Won't writers, whose responsibility is to constantly reinvent language, free language, break it down, and reconstitute it in provoking, instructive, entertaining ways, perform similar magic on sports? Will poets shame us into recognizing that sport does as much to perpetuate racial and gender stereotyping as it does to cure these evils?

Sports are like sonnets. Sonnets are like sports. In other words, sport is to *play* as sonnets are to *language*. In one form or another everybody plays. Sport refines, regulates, intensifies, communalizes the drama and fun inherent in play. Everybody employs language in one form or another. Poetry refines, regulates, intensifies, communalizes the drama and fun inherent in language.

Writing stories and playing hoop attract me, excite me, liberate me for many of the same reasons: you never know what's going to happen next; your previous performances don't count in the tally of today's game; each outing begins as a sort of blank slate; the opportunity to play, to compete is what's most precious; process matters more than product. I could continue the parallel, but I'd just be telling the story from a fiction writer's point of view, and you've promised me poets, so I'm getting out of the way.

Next. Who's next? as we say on the playground.

John Edgar Wideman

Preface

Sports are now one of the few places where the American ideal of a melting pot occurs, in full public view, on a daily basis. We are quite a long way from the days when sports were sandlot folly for young men. Now several of the top players in the NBA are from Africa, Croatia, Serbia, and elsewhere. Some of the best snowboarders in America are Japanese, while the top surfers are from all around the world. The WNBA is growing into a marketing and entertainment force. From the overachieving underdog, to the breaking of racial barriers, to the fan vicariously slugging from the bleachers, to the creation of the professional athlete, to the lone amateur shadowboxing around his room, this anthology is a celebration of the history, development, and diversity of sports *and* poetry. Great poets, seduced by the movement and drama in sport, have tried to duplicate its rhythms and timings in their poems.

A sense of timing, lyricism, and drama are not unique to the sports poem, but they become immediate issues when one starts to discuss the urgencies of a body in motion. The adrenaline of sports is something a poet must confront: the way time slows as the heart speeds, or, if the player or poet is off his game, the way time does not slow as the heart does not speed, and he misses a catch.

Take a look at Christopher Merrill's "A Boy Juggling a Soccer Ball," for example: the sharp descriptions, the staggered line breaks and lengths, the alternating rhythms stop-time us on a summer afternoon not gone by. Or look at Yusef Komunyakaa's "Slam, Dunk, & Hook." We pump fake and drop step around players with Sonny Boy while he tries to soar over his mother's death. Sports and poetry are not just entertainment but attempts to make sense of and rise above human suffering.

I hate to limit a reading of these poems in any way. But it might be helpful to point out that among the many parallels made between sports, poetry, and life, this idea of transcendence is inherent — the idea of rising above some invisible boundary on the court as well as the page. Stephen Dunn discusses this phenomenon best in his essay "Basketball and Poetry: The Two Richies" from his book *Walking Light*:

Perhaps basketball and poetry have just a few things in common, but the most important is the possibility of transcendence. The opposite is labor. In writing, every writer knows when he or she is laboring to achieve an effect. You want to get from here to there, but you find yourself willing it, forcing it. The equivalent in basketball is aiming your shot, a kind of strained and usually ineffective purposefulness. What you want to be is in some kind of flow, each next moment a discovery. Unconscious? Maybe, but more accurately a movement toward higher consciousness, of saying what you didn't know you could say, propelled by the mysteries of the process.

It was Charles Simic who said that if you want to know what was going on in a culture at any given time, read the poets. Poets write about the subjects available to them. Sports have become hard to avoid in our daily lives, especially if we watch television, listen to the radio, or live in a city. These poems give feeling and sense to a society obsessed with records and numbers; they make the heightened moments of the amateur or fan or professional anything but fleeting. Sports have become one of America's means to account for time passing, for days spent in cubicles, or, as Bob Teschek, an organizer of endurance races, put it, "Most modern Americans are bored to tears, so they need a challenge. It used to be work or your daily life, now it's sport." Sports are a contemporary answer to Prufrock's "muttering about the room." And the writing of a poem changes the dynamic of watching or remembering a game from passive to active. These poems take the billboards and highlights and empty ice rinks and give them a presence, make them speak.

A disproportionate number of the poems included here concern baseball, America's "national pastime." (Walt Whitman is reported to have loved baseball until the pitchers began throwing overhand so that the hitters could not hit the ball, the meanest thing he thought they could do.) In the last thirty years, though, as basketball and boxing and football have been popularized, more poems have been written about them. And as golf becomes accessible to all, and the so-called fringe sports like skateboarding and surfing and rock climbing appear in the Olympics and on ESPN, I expect more poems to be written about them too.

I have used this popularity formula to define what is or is not a sports-related poem. That is, if the sport is played in the Olympics or shown on a sports networks like ESPN, I have determined the poem to be about a "legitimate" sport. This means that the parameters for what qualifies as a sports-related poem have been expanded while being focused on, but not limited to, an adult audience.

By definition, any time there is change, there is an exchange of energy. The poems in this anthology do not disobey this law of physics. The energy and movement of the sports-related poem first attracted me to it, and I have tried to maintain that energy and movement throughout this anthology: the energy and movement of a boy fly-fishing after his father dies; two girls ice-skating at dusk; a boy juggling a soccer ball for hours by himself; basketball players blowing layups with no time on the clock; a famous football player ending his career in a heroin haze; an amateur runner completing a marathon; a young man struggling with ideas of masculinity as he watches a boxing match with several other men; a young woman using boxing as metaphor for everything gone wrong in a relationship; a son accessing memories of his father the only way he can, through baseball; an old man remembering what it was like to rise above a basketball rim; a widow remembering her husband's race car crash; a boxer knocked down who gets back up because he is sure he can take it, sure he can win. This anthology is a celebration of everyone who has participated in the shimmy and shake and sweat of poetry, of sports.

motion

Pumping Iron

DIANE ACKERMAN

She doesn't want
the bunchy look
of male lifters:
torso an unyielding love-knot,
arms hard at mid-boil.
Doesn't want
the dancing bicepses
of pros.
Just to run her flesh
up the flagpole
of her body,
to pull her roaming flab
into tighter cascades,
machete a waist
through the jungle
of her hips,
a trim waist
two hands might grip
as a bouquet.

Event

KIM ADDONIZIO

The small arena almost filled,
the vendors pulling foamy beer
from rows of taps,

around the ring the long tables
of judges and sportswriters,
the bald promoter,

a photographer leaning in,
one elbow on the canvas to catch
a glove at the precise moment

it connects, the microphones carrying
the smack of leather up through wires,
satellites, into living rooms

though the spectators in the back
can't hear it,
or the man in the twelfth row listening

to the three behind him, cursing
the fighter this man has money on —
Nigger, pussy, fucking bum —

until the man turns around with
Shut the fuck up
and grabs one by the hair,

the two struggling briefly
as the crowd absorbs them
and settles them down.

Now the two knocks announcing ten seconds
to the end of the round; they stagger
to separate corners for comfort

and advice, icy water poured
down the silk shorts of one, chilled
metal held to the other's blossoming eye,

his good one following the ring girl
climbing in, holding aloft the time left
as she circles in her dangerous spiked heels

and white strip of bathing suit
to whistles and applause.
If you're waiting for more than this —

the names of the fighters, say,
or the outcome of the match, a decision
no one will agree with,

that will enter the record
of losses and temporary victories,
of the body's weight each struggles to maintain,

if you're waiting for the girl
to lie down under you
and moan your own name

in some damp corner of your dreams,
then you know why you're here
and why I can't tell you anything.

You know why you're aching
and have to keep taking it,
you recognize that roaring in your ears.

Late Round

KIM ADDONIZIO

When the fighters slow down, moving towards each other
as though underwater, gloves laboring to rise
before their faces, each punch followed by a clutch
when they hold on like exhausted lovers,
I think of us in the last months, and of the night
you stood in my kitchen, drunk, throwing wild combinations
at the air, at something between us that would not
go down. I watch the two of them
planted in that ring, unable to trust their legs,
the bell's reprieve suspended in some impossible distance,
and I remember my voice, cursing our life together
until there was nothing either one of us would fight for.
These men, you'd say, have heart — they keep on,
though neither remembers his strategy
or hears the shouts from his corner. And it's true
you had more heart than I did, until that night
you gave us up, finally, and dropped crying to your knees
on my kitchen floor. The fighters stagger and fall together,
flailing against the ropes. They embrace
and are separated, but they don't let go.

Narrative: Ali

ELIZABETH ALEXANDER

a poem in twelve rounds

Narrative

1.   My head so big
they had to pry
me out. I'm sorry
Bird (is what I call
my mother). Cassius
Marcellus Clay,
Muhammad Ali;
you can say
my name in any
language, any
continent: Ali.

2.   Two photographs
of Emmett Till,
born my year,
on my birthday.
One, he's smiling,
happy, and the other one
is after. His mother
did the bold thing,
kept the casket open,
made the thousands look upon
his bulging eyes,
his twisted neck,
her lynched black boy.
I couldn't sleep
for thinking,
Emmett Till.

One day I went
down to the train tracks,
found some iron
shoe-shine rests
and planted them
between the ties
and waited
for a train to come,
and watched the train
derail, and ran,
and after that
I slept at night.

3.   I need to train
around people,
hear them talk,
talk back. I need
to hear the traffic,
see people in
the barbershop,
people getting
shoeshines, talking,
hear them talk,
talk back.

4.   Bottom line: Olympic gold
can't buy a black man
a Louisville hamburger
in nineteen-sixty.

Wasn't even real gold.
I watched the river
drag the ribbon down,
red, white, and blue.

5. Laying on the bed,
   praying for a wife,
   in walk Sonji Roi.

   Pretty little shape.
   Do you like
   chop suey?

   Can I wash your hair
   underneath
   that wig?

   Lay on the bed,
   Girl. Lie
   with me.

   Shake to the east,
   to the north,
   south, west —

   but remember,
   remember, I need
   a Muslim wife. So

   Quit using lipstick.
   Quit your boogaloo.
   Cover up your knees

   like a Muslim
   wife, religion,
   religion, a Muslim

   wife. Eleven
   months with Sonji,
   first woman I loved.

6.   There's not
      too many days
      that pass that I
      don't think
      of how it started,
      but I know
      no Great White Hope
      can beat
      a true black champ.
      Jerry Quarry
      could have been
      a movie star,
      a millionaire,
      a Senator,
      a President —
      he only had
      to do one thing,
      is whip me,
      but he can't.

7.   *Dressing Room Visitor*
      He opened
      up his shirt:
      "KKK" cut
      in his chest.
      He dropped
      his trousers:
      latticed scars
      where testicles
      should be. His face
      bewildered, frozen,
      in the Alabama woods
      that night in 1966
      when they left him

for dead, his testicles
in a Dixie cup.
You a warning,
they told him,
to smart-mouth,
sassy-acting niggers,
meaning niggers
still alive,
meaning any nigger,
meaning niggers
like me.

8.   *Training*
      Unsweetened grapefruit juice
      will melt my stomach down.
      Don't drive if you can walk,
      don't walk if you can run.
      I add a mile each day
      and run in eight-pound boots.

      My knuckles sometimes burst
      the glove. I let dead skin
      build up, and then I peel it,
      let it scar, so I don't bleed
      as much. My bones
      absorb the shock.

      I train in three-minute
      spurts, like rounds: three
      rounds big bag, three speed
      bag, three jump rope, one
      minute breaks,
      no more, no less.

Am I too old? Eat only
kosher meat. Eat cabbage,
carrots, beets, and watch
the weight come down:
two-thirty, two-twenty,
two-ten, two-oh-nine.

9.   Will I go
like Kid Paret,
a fractured
skull, a ten-day
sleep, dreaming
alligators, pork-
chops, saxophones,
slow grinds, funk,
fishbowls, lightbulbs,
bats, typewriters,
tuning forks, funk,
clocks, red rubber
ball, what you see
in that lifetime
knockout minute
on the cusp?
You could be
let go,
you could be
snatched back.

10.   *Rumble in the Jungle*
Ali boma ye,
Ali boma ye,
means kill him, Ali,
which is different
from a whupping
which is what I give,
but I lead them chanting

anyway, *Ali*
boma ye, because
here in Africa
black people fly
planes and run countries.

I'm still making up
for the foolishness
I said when I was
Clay from Louisville,
where I learned Africans
lived naked in straw
huts eating tiger meat,
grunting and grinning,
swinging from vines,
pounding their chests —

I pound my chest but of my own accord.

11.　I said to Joe Frazier,
　　　first thing, get a good house
　　　in case you get crippled
　　　so you and your family
　　　can sleep somewhere. Always
　　　keep one good Cadillac.
　　　And watch how you dress
　　　with that cowboy hat,
　　　pink suits, white shoes —
　　　that's how pimps dress,
　　　or kids, and you a champ,
　　　or wish you were, 'cause
　　　I can whip you in the ring
　　　or whip you in the street.
　　　Now back to clothes,
　　　wear dark clothes, suits,
　　　black suits, like you the best

at what you do, like you
President of the World.
Dress like that.
Put them yellow pants away.
We dinosaurs gotta
look good, gotta sound
good, gotta be good,
the greatest, that's what
I told Joe Frazier,
and he said to me,
we both bad niggers.
We don't do no crawlin'.

12.   They called me "the fistic pariah."

They said I didn't love my country,
called me a race-hater, called me out
of my name, waited for me
to come out on a streetcar, shot at me,
hexed me, cursed me, wished me
all manner of ill-will,
told me I was finished.

Here I am,
like the song says,
come and take me,

"The People's Champ,"

myself,
Muhammad.

Penance

SHERMAN ALEXIE

I remember sun-
days when the man I
call my father made

me shoot free throws, one
for every day of my life
so far. I remember
the sin of imperfect

spin, the ball falling in-
to that moment between
a father and forgive-

ness, between the hands reach-
ing up and everything
they can possibly hold.

Why We Play Basketball

SHERMAN ALEXIE

[handwritten: cold]

[handwritten margin notes: 5v5 bball / Quintain 5 syllables]

1. In December, snow
   covered the court. We
   wrapped our hands in old
   socks, soaked the white snow
   with kerosene, lit

   the match, and melted it
   all down to pavement.
   We were Indians
   who wanted to play
   basketball. Nothing

   could stop us from that,
   not the hunger in
   our thin bellies, not
   the fear of missed shots,
   not the threat of white

   snow. We were small boys
   who would grow into
   small men. We played ball
   until dark, then played
   until we could see

   neither hoop nor ball.
   We played until our
   mothers and fathers
   came searching for us
   and carried us home.

2. We play because we
    remember the first
    time we shot the ball
    and knew, beyond doubt,
    as it floated toward

    the hoop, that it was
    going to be good.
    We walked off the court,
    left the ball waiting
    as we fell in love

    with Indian girls
    who grew past us, who
    grew into Indian
    women. Somehow, we
    grew families while

    that ball waited, in-
    ert, suspended, till
    we remembered, with
    a complex rush of
    pain and joy, what we'd

    left behind, how we
    loved the ball as it
    finally dropped in-
    to the net, after
    years of such patience.

3. We wanted to know
    who was best, who could
    change the game into
    something new. We knew
    about Seymour. Blind

    See-more

and deaf, he played by
sense of smell. Leather
balls drove him crazy.
He identified
his teammates by tribe:

Spokanes smelled like bread;
Flatheads smelled like pine;
Colville smelled like snow;
Lester smelled like wine.
Seymour shot the ball

when the wind told him
it was time to shoot.
In basketball, we
find enough reasons
to believe in God,

or something smaller
than God. We believe
in Seymour, who holds
the ball in his hands
like you hold your God.

4.   It is just a game
we are told by those
who cannot play it
unless it is play.
For us, it is war,

often desperate
and without reason.
We throw our body
against another
body. We learn to

hate each other, hate
the ball, hate the hoop,
hate the fallen snow,
hate our clumsy hands,
hate our thirsty mouths

when we drink from
the fountain. We hate
our fathers. We hate
our mothers. We hate
the face in our mirror.

We play basketball
because we want to
separate love from
hate, and because we
know how to keep score.

5. We play basketball
because we still love
the place where we lived.
It was a small house
with one door. We lived

there for twenty years
with crazy cousins
and one basketball.
We fought over it
constantly. I climbed

into a tall tree
with the ball, refused
to come down unless
they made me captain.
My brother dragged me

from the tree and punched
me so hard I saw
red horses. We play
because we believe
in our skins and hands.

These hands hold the ball.
These hands hold the tribe.
These hands build fires.
We are a small tribe.
We build small fires.

The Jogger on
Riverside Drive, 5:00 A.M.

AGHA SHAHID ALI

The dark scissors of his legs
cut the moon's

raw silk, highways of wind
torn into lanes, his feet

pushing down the shadow
whose patterns he becomes

while trucks, one by one,
pass him by,

headlights pouring
from his face, his eyes

cracked as the Hudson
wraps street lamps

in its rippled blue shells,
the summer's thin, thin veins

bursting with dawn,
he, now suddenly free,

from the air, from himself,
his heart beating far, far

behind him.

To Satch

SAM ALLEN

Sometimes I feel like I will *never* stop
Just go on forever
Till one fine mornin
I'm gonna reach up and grab me a handfulla stars
Swing out my long lean leg
And whip three hot strikes burnin down the heavens
And look over at God and say
How about that!

The career of Satchel Paige, the legendary baseball pitcher,
extended into five decades.

Locker Room Etiquette

CRAIG ARNOLD

Please refrain from frankly ogling your neighbor's
penis or buttocks. This goes without saying —
bear in mind, however, that the simplest
    courtesy often

is the first forgotten. Likewise, the appraising ·
sidelong gaze, however surreptitious,
seldom fails to offend when it is noticed.
    Wandering eyes are

best averted. The small talk that in other
awkward situations would ease the moment
here you should avoid addressing to strangers,
    even familiar

faces, who often find it quite disarming.
This is neither the time nor place for idle
chitchat, or to broach uncertain topics —
    keep to the distance

run, the merits of this or that equipment,
warm-ups, weights, reps, heart rates, soreness of muscles.
Comments, however, on your own or your fellows'
    sweaty aroma

rarely are welcomed. Modesty and its over-
balance, in this respect, are equal, drawing
too much attention. Take, as an example,
    running the gauntlet

locker to shower, a source of so much worry.
Should one promenade the flower of manhood
fearlessly down the hall, or wear one's towel
    prudishly knotted

over the flanks, only to find it twirling
down to the ankles, forcing one to postures
neither becoming nor graceful to retrieve it?
    Strive for a balance:

walk at a steady clip, the towel loosely
draped over the shoulder. If necessary,
practice in front of a mirror. Where nakedness makes you
    shy as a hermit

crab between shells, or a snail who hides his
tremulous horns at the first smell of danger,
summon about yourself an impenetrable
    aura, an armor,

over which the playful spray of the shower
spatters harmlessly. Spare the soap, and lather
only as much as may fulfill the barest
    dictates of hygiene,

lingering nowhere long, except the armpits,
also in drying, with an unspecific
sweep over crotch, the peach-crease of the buttocks.
    Carry your person

stiffly, as if each limb required a heroic
effort of will to flex — your head should never
drop below the armpit, or only briefly
    tying your laces.

Handle yourself at all times with distasteful
resignation, as one regards an oyster
slick on the half-shell. Maybe it is better
    not to imagine

oysters, or snails. Those were bad examples.
Try to forget them. Reticence in thought as
well as speech will keep your attention focused
    here in the moment,

far away from that boy on the bench directly
opposite — yes, the one that you've been sitting
naked silently beside in the sauna —
    look at your toenails,

stretch your hamstrings, think of how you are lifting
more each day, soon you'll be pressing sixty,
seventy, eighty pounds, up to the weight of
    nobody watching.

A Dream of the Ring:
The Great Jack Johnson

GEORGE BARLOW

I'll be the first
to chase the white hope
from coast to coast
corner him at last
& buckle his knees
Rednecks in Reno
will check in their guns
& drop their ducats
to watch the sun gleam
from my teeth my dark muscles
my great bald head
Vamps & debs will blush & giggle
as they watch me train
will prance into paradise with me
carve their lives in my back
fan themselves
knead my heart like dough
Hate will snag me
jail me for crossing state lines
& being a man
I'll fight bulls in Madrid
Griots will feed me to their children
to make them strong
My jabs & hooks
sweat & knockouts
my derbies long cars & gall
will live forever
I'll have one rag of a time
when I become Jack Johnson

Called Up: Tinker to Evers to Chance

DOROTHY BARRESI

In three weeks he will be back down talking
drunk in the Econo Lodge
off Sugar Creek Road,

as reported by the *Charlotte Observer*: vowing return.
Not enough heat, pepper, punch & judy.
Occasional hits in the wheelhouse,

but clearly not knocking
the wide moon out of round over Baltimore
or bleary-eyed, noble Detroit.

Luck throws its change-up.
Luck, the old timers say, and who should know better,
with their colons and bum tickers,

their failing vision of which tears are the by-product
in spring when azaleas
and baseball bloom,

luck could throw a lambchop past a wolf.
So it does. It's true. Now
admit it's the very same food chain of love — self-love and self-pity —

we rattle each day
as a weak kind of answer, snarling it
down to the bone with our hungers. We're *still* hungry

for more than words in our mouths. For once,
we want not to be
so replaceable. So the shortstop

is smart in his own dumbfounded way.
He's wearing the gold cross and gold chain
his mother, Lupe, sent last winter

from the Dominican Republic.
He isn't asking any tough questions.
When his name is picked apart

by the P.A.'s rickety static, then boomed
over red clay basepaths
and tobacco barns slotted open

to catch the killer sun,
and Neatsfoot Oil making the gloves glisten and the ball
smack! smack! like ripe, dangerous

fruit in their hands,
he sails his cap high up: the thing wanted —
it was all *worth* wanting. As for what will hurt him

must cruelly in the end, hope
ending or hope beginning
all over again like some cosmic, half-baked

karmic plan for winning
despite the cost,
it's academic, really. It's in the air like sweat, or smoke,

or pine tar pitch,
or that other story we keep feeding ourselves.
The one about the bug being born

into the body of the president, and
later, into a gleaming white twenty-gallon hat.

It's never too early for regret.
Look. Already the crowd is singing "Rocky Top," and swaying
as the great, right boy who's grinning

sneezes once, waves
back to the wartime geezers – adios! –
then runs down the dugout steps and out of sight.

Lifting

DOROTHY BARRESI

If muscles are the currency of dreams,
you are flesh life
curator of the New World, bowing
to nothing but these iron notes.
Sweat, heft, shoulder, thigh, lunge.
Because you wear yourself like a suit
I could never afford, my arms
strain and pretend.
My breath falls through its own trapdoor.

I who have said, *let the thing be what it is.*
Who fed popular children
coins of attention, held down
the cowed corners of my eighth-grade dances.
Who was born like all homely girls
old enough to know better —
I asked you once
what was it like to grow up handsome,
meaning loved. Just now

I've forgotten your answer.
In this garage, where wrecked cans of motor oil
compete with garden tools
for a dying season,
you row the silver barbell up
and I'm meant to see everything injures.
The speed bag is a teardrop
coming back too fast, the heavy bag
a punch-drunk promise,
Everlast in bright red letters.

If a man bench-pressing twice his weight
could lift himself and one other
up, safe above all harm —
but he cannot. One night
on the right-hand side of smoke,
our bodies set out for their true country.
Our bones will collapse, one into the other,
mine into yours as
cheap traveling cups do.

Take a sip. That was my mother
pressing a glass of water into my hands
and the words as she knelt by my bed
were told to comfort.
Her story was simple and thus lost on me,
all about an ugly duckling and a guardian angel
with a funny sense of timing.

I remember her tone, *forbear,*
her face haggard with love as she said it.
But what if the articulate stands
in front of us now, golden and flexing,
bored as any god?
All our years in a hard won mirror!
Reverse transcendence,
I keep lifting,
vow I am almost ready to put foolish things down.

Slow

MARVIN BELL

I go out to find whatever comes
but the first fifteen minutes
are for trying to breathe, the next
fifteen for using both legs
without almost having to count
cadence, and the second half hour
for water, two cheeps at a bird,
and the reassurance that important chemicals
are now in the bloodstream. The first
fifteen minutes are the hardest,
anyone will tell you that, the first thirty
are the hardest, and the first hour
is the hardest hour, but in the second hour
something goes right without your knowing:
a mixture of good motions, oxygen
and a certain giving-up
that permits you not to hurry
and gives you back for every slow minute
two that are beyond you. It's the slow
who have to keep going who get to take back
the possessive note they struck
when they were strong. Weak, they find
fatigue is buoyant, they can coast, float,
and they sometimes have thoughts
too pure to be brought home
but not righter than others, despite
what you see on the talk shows
with your legs up and your toenails blacker.
Out-and-back runs, says David,
are like folding a piece of paper.
At the far end, you know what to do.
Loops are the worst, repeating what you see

as if you owned it. You look forward
to the past; the run lengthens.
I like runs that take a hill in one direction,
pass a body of water,
go down one street no one knows,
and find a breeze. Most of us save the long run
for Sunday, which is sensible
not religious. No believer, after all,
but no doubter, I do
look around, except uphill, the more so
after the first two hours
(when it gets easier).

What They Do to You in Distant Places

MARVIN BELL

I never told you.
There was a woman — in the greening season
of a tropical island
where I had gone to break some hard thoughts
across my knee
and also, although I am no athlete
but breathe with my stomach like the satyr
and live in my stomach
according to bile and acid and bread and bitter chocolate,
to run a long race for the first time.
On that morning,
it was raining in great screens
of the purest water and almost no one at 4 A.M.
where I waited, half-sheltered
by the edge of my dark hotel, for a let-up.
Except her, suddenly
from nowhere — smelling of long hair and dew,
smelling of dew and grass and a little powder.
She wore a dress that moved.
She had been out dancing and the night and she
were young.
I wore a black watch cap like an old sailor
but I was all there was.

I said no, I had to do something else.
She asked how far? And
if I would run all that way — hours.
I said I'd try,
and then she kissed me for luck
and her mouth on mine was as sweet as the wild guava
and the smell of her hair
was that of the little bit of dew the lover

brings home from the park
when again she shows up in the morning.
I don't know where I have been
that I have ever had such a kiss
that asked nothing and gave everything.
I walked out into the rain
as if blessed. But I had forgotten
what they do to you in distant places,
taking away your memory
before sending you back. You and me.
I confess,
I forgot her within the hour
in the gross odors of my labors.
If I had known what she was doing . . .
Perhaps she's with you now.

The Fish

ELIZABETH BISHOP

[handwritten margin notes: "beauty in aging" and "use of similes"]

I caught a tremendous fish
and held him beside the boat
half out of water, with my hook
fast in a corner of his mouth.
He didn't fight.
He hadn't fought at all.
He hung a grunting weight,
battered and venerable
and homely. Here and there
his brown skin hung in strips
like ancient wallpaper,
and its pattern of darker brown
was like wallpaper:
shapes like full-blown roses
stained and lost through age.
He was speckled with barnacles,
fine rosettes of lime,
and infested
with tiny white sea-lice,
and underneath two or three
rags of green weed hung down.
While his gills were breathing in
the terrible oxygen
— the frightening gills,
fresh and crisp with blood,
that can cut so badly —
I thought of the coarse white flesh
packed in like feathers,
the big bones and the little bones,
the dramatic reds and blacks
of his shiny entrails,
and the pink swim-bladder

like a big peony.
I looked into his eyes
which were far larger than mine
but shallower, and yellowed,
the irises backed and packed
with tarnished tinfoil
seen through the lenses
of old scratched isinglass.
They shifted a little, but not
to return my stare.
— It was more like the tipping
of an object toward the light.
I admired his sullen face,
the mechanism of his jaw,
and then I saw
that from his lower lip
— if your could call it a lip —
grim, wet, and weaponlike,
hung five old pieces of fish-line,
or four and a wire leader
with the swivel still attached,
with all their five big hooks
grown firmly in his mouth.
A green line, frayed at the end
where he broke it, two heavier lines,
and a fine black thread
still crimped from the strain and snap
when it broke and he got away.
Like medals with their ribbons
frayed and wavering,
a five-haired beard of wisdom
trailing from his aching jaw.
I stared and stared
and victory filled up
the little rented boat,
from the pool of bilge

where oil had spread a rainbow
around the rusted engine
to the bailer rusted orange,
the sun-cracked thwarts,
the oarlocks on their strings,
the gunnels — until everything
was rainbow, rainbow, rainbow!
And I let the fish go.

Water & Light

NOAH BLAUSTEIN

It was too soon
To think of her passing,
So I passed
Evenings in the water.

I wanted to look
Like a boy out for a surf
And go from a boy
To a shadow

Against the colored horizon
And from a shadow
To being the sun, a part of the sun
As it slipped over the other side.

I was happy enough,
On clear days,
To float
And see a "bottom" underneath me.

I forgot
Waves.
I forgot
The shore.

Sand shifted in the undercurrent
Along the bottom and,
As the sun got lower,
Clear water turned

Into the purples and oranges of reflection
And my wetsuit
Became a part
Of that reflection.

As the sky went black, slowly,
The water went black,
Slowly, and I lost sight
Of my feet.

I lost sense
Of what moved beneath me,
I lost track
Of what swelled towards me.

Decisions by instinct.
That was fear.

Cold water, sitting on the edge of light,
The willful deprivation of sense –

My Baptist friend says
"You were trying to cross over,
To get as close to her as you could
Without leaving entirely."

On shore, shadows
Shifting through trash cans,
The sound of santa anas drying leaves,
Brought me back.

On shore, I changed quickly:
Stripped my wetsuit into puddles
Of headlights on the highway,
Let the wind mix the salt into my brow.

Rodeo Tangent

KENDRA BORGMANN

Woman in front of you's black hair blowing over itself – some man loves
this hair – did she wash it last night – did she rinse with cool water –
was her wedding band on – has a bee ever tangled in it – was she
drinking beer – did she throw a fit or calmly shake it out – does her
jewelry snag in it – does he ever wash it – does he leave his ring on –
is it on when he bales hay – shoes horses – does he wonder what she'd
look like with yellow hair – does he prefer it down – does he notice
when it throws back light – does the sun seep to the roots – does it
scorch his fingers like just ironed cotton – does her cowboy hat slip off
– who trims the back – do the damp pieces fall with a click to the floor
– how long was it when they first met – were they kids – did he yank it –
did she hate his guts – does she have bald dreams – someone has cut it
with the green handled grass clippers – would he still find her beautiful
– have other men touched it – did they recover – is one of them down
there speed tying a calf – is her husband better at it – would he pass a
blind smell test – if ten heads of long hair were lined up would he pick
hers without hesitation – what would swirl up inside him – does he find
her strands in his work jacket – does he pull them out one at a time –
does he watch them float to the ground – do trees have her hair in them
– do nests – which birds has she kept warm – when she lies on him –
does her hair fall forward – does it hide her breasts – does it get in his
mouth – does he hold it back – does the night smell like yarrow crushed
underfoot –

Playing Basketball with the Viet Cong

KEVIN BOWEN

for Nguyên Quang Sáng

You never thought it would come to this,
that afternoon in the war
when you leaned so hard into the controls
you almost became part of the landscape:
just you, the old man, old woman
and their buffalo.
You never thought then
that this grey-haired man in sandals
smoking Gauloises on your back porch,
drinking your beer, his rough cough
punctuating tales of how he fooled
the French in '54,
would arrive at your back door
to call you out to shoot some baskets, friend.
If at first he seems awkward,
before long he's got it down.
His left leg lifts from the ground,
his arms arch back then forward
from the waist to release the ball
arcing to the hoop, one, two, . . .
ten straight times. You stare at him
in his tee shirt, sandals, and shorts.
Yes, he smiles. It's a gift,
good for bringing gunships down
as he did in the Delta
and in other places where, he whispers,
there may be other scores to settle.

Dove at Sundown

CATHERINE BOWMAN

for Valerie

There's a caliche pit not far from here
where the dove at sundown go to drink.

I'm told to camouflage myself in shades
of live oak, scrubby cedar, and mesquite.

On the way we break to scrutinize
a band of turkey roosting in a draw:

that's a dried-out river of smooth, round stones
that takes the rain in thunderstorms and floods.

The pickup slows and butts us through the bump
gates. Then we pass a row of molasses licks:

troughs of sticky sorghum for the Brahma,
the Black Angus, and the goats to tongue.

The cattle horses here are all neck-reiners:
to steer one, touch the reins against the neck.

Bitterweed: cows bloat on those sour leaves.
Spike: a whitetail deer with deformed horns.

The exotics: fallow and axis,
deer imported from another continent

who wander down in search of food and water
from the big game ranches to the north.

Here the sky's your basic working blue.
And there's oil, big pockets of natural gas,

and the oil from the sheared angora.
Thirty years of stuffing greasy mohair

into burlap bags has made that weathered
goat man's hands as soft as little girls'.

Now at the pit the heat's alive and layered:
body heat, fever heat, blood heat.

The trick to killing dove is to anticipate
their flight and shoot in that blank space.

The earth is silent and aflame. Except
for the metallic drill of some weird species.

We clean our kill by headlight. First you twist
the head off like a bottle cap. The thumb

and pointer finger are used as hooks
to disengage guts and any shot.

I'm surprised how warm they are inside.
Blood splatters on my face and shirt.

We marinate the birds in cheap Bordeaux
and stuff each one with sage and jalapeño.

Our bellies full, we strip down and soak
in a cleaned-out cow tank swimming pool.

Faceup and floating underneath the stars,
we watch the bombers from the nearby base,

out for test flights: slow and prehistoric,
petroglyphs of winged jaguars come to life.

My Knicks Are Going to Beat Your Spurs — NBA Souvenir Bracelet 1999 for My Long Distance Love

CATHERINE BOWMAN

Spursknicksspursknicksspursknicksspursknicksspurskni
cksspursknicksspursknicksspursknicksspursknicksspurs
knicksspursknicksspursknicksspursknicksspursknickssp
ursknicksspursknicksspursknicksspursknicksspursknick

spursknicks		spursknic
ksspursknic	j	ksspurskn
icksspurskn	a	icksspursk
nicksspursk	n	nicksspurs
knicksspurs	jingle	knicksspur
sknicksspur	l	sknicksspu
rsknicksspu	e	rsknickssp
ursknickssp		ursknickss
pursknickss		pursknicks
spursknicks		spursknick

sspursknicksspursknicksspursknicksspursknickspurskni
cksspursknicksspursknicksspursknicksspursknickspursk
nicksspursknicksspursknicksspursknicksspursknickspur
sknicksspursknicksspursknickspursknicksspursknickssp
ursknicksspursknicksspursknickspursknicksspursknicks

43

Fishing in Winter

RALPH BURNS

A man staring at a small lake sees
his father cast light line out over
the willows. He's forgotten his
father has been dead for two years
and the lake is where a blue fog
rolls, and the sky could be, if it
were black or blue or white,
the backdrop of all attention.

He wades out to join the father,
following where the good strikes
seem to lead. It's cold. The shape
breath takes on a cold day is like
anything else — a rise on a small lake,
the Oklahoma hills, blue scrub —
a shape already inside a shape,
two songs, two breaths on the water.

Memory

RALPH BURNS

Didn't think of the clasp
or stirrup, that cartilage
beckoning the knee, surrounding it
and leading to cap and musculature, not
the physics but the metaphysics —
heat and side-ways light — that fluid motion,
grace of my old man a little younger
than I am now; did I think of that
hatch and latch, sinking too;
did I think of that ache of pleasure
at wondering at myself age, not realizing
years later,
this persistence, dull all right,
radiates differently.
Didn't I think of something
during that casual golf swing
feeling a catch or twinge
minutes later, or remember that years ago
I could have tended a bruise like a fire,
lilted over pain — my lyric elegy,
that elegiac lyric — ;
didn't I think of something almost accidental
like that sweet swing
lifting over the trees,
if I could only retrace that movement in the body,
that circular plane
perfect and unrehearsed.
I put the ball on the tee.
That catch doesn't come until later.
I think of it as death,
self-inflicted, and I'm wrong.
I search with my fingers for that tendon,

elastic mass making action possible,
that sharp inheritance, that impulse
under the skin prompting its hinge,
protuberant in cypresses
long in water, brought down
by force. Under cardboard, under
that bright bridge of concrete and steel,
under stars, under abutment and buttress,
arch and leaf brown as my old father's eyes,
under a traffic blowing by —
I dream of my son who bends
in the knees out of joy, William
out of the wild time unseen, sweet flower
of improvisation.

Russ Joy Little League

DOUGLAS CARLSON

God help me, liberal mothers,
I'm trying not to be competitive:

standing apart from the screaming others,
a quiet smile on my lips, bemused,
watching children play, striking
the pose of former athlete
reduced to jogging and tennis,
thickening around the middle.

But there we are, Kevin, you
are two-for-two; I am oh-for-thirty-seven,
last inning, runner on second.

You take the first pitch for a strike;
the banshees howl from the bleachers
and a small word passes through your
half smile. But you are angry with
yourself, not the umpire. I'm just proud.

The second pitch is high;
you swing in anger as I
would have done. Now we have
two strikes on us.
I'm trying not to be competitive,
but we must protect the plate:
two strikes, two outs,
last inning, the sun is in our eyes.
There will be better times than these.

Now I want to be with you
in our fantasies: a compact, level
swing, the ball sailing like a gull
out and over the falling sun
to a jetty where we sit growing older,
not competing with fish we never catch.

Capper Kaplinski at the North Side Cue Club

HAYDEN CARRUTH

What's it like? You take it from me,
      kid, the old dinger don't
raise up like he used to for a
      squint at every nice grownt-

up piece moseying down the main,
      not no more — no, sir. But
it ain't so bad. Wasn't nothing
      but a pain in your nut

anyways when he used to pop
      up all the time with no-
where to put him, nothing but grief,
      the same old crazy go-

round, don't think I don't remember.
      By the Jesus, boy, it
ain't so bad at all without all
      that, specially since a tit

still gives me a real good feeling,
      but like it's mental, not
in the gut, you understand? So
      I see some young broad trot-

ting along the asphalt hurry-
      ing somewheres, her boobs jig-
ging a little under her sweat-
      er, nice and not too big,

now ain't that a good sight to see?
          No question. You bet your
ass. Why, it makes me feel warm like,
          like sunshine all over

and me up setting on a bench
          in Hillside Park just watch-
ing the kids skim them saucers, or
          the girls doing hopscotch,

or anything, it don't matter,
          just so it's spring and a
sunny afternoon. What I mean
          I can still glom onto

the things that make life worth living
          and sex still has something
to do with it, and always will,
          even if I ain't been

too sharp at explaining. Life's a
          doozy, that's how I see
it. Well, this here's called nine-ball. Is
          we playing or ain't we?

The Catch

RAYMOND CARVER

Happy to have these fish!
In spite of the rain, they came
to the surface and took
the No. 14 Black Mosquito.
He had to concentrate,
close everything else out
for a change. His old life,
which he carried around
like a pack. And the new one,
that one too. Time and again
he made what he felt were the most
intimate of human movements.
Strained his heart to see
the difference between a raindrop
and a brook trout. Later,
walking across the wet field
to the car. Watching
the wind change the aspen trees.
He abandoned everyone
he once loved.

Moorer Denies Holyfield in Twelve

OLENA KALYTIAK DAVIS

Caesar's Palace.
The way life keeps splitting itself in two.

Twenty four hours later Florida
had pushed itself under
the wheels of our white Olds.
My father getting out
of the car. I'm squinting, his
shirt is that bright.

I was stunned for a minute
but was able to clear my head.

I'm on the phone now, trying to keep this front
from moving over his white cloud of a head,
because my father used to be two men,
but now he's old.

One minute you're talking weather. Then,
a nasty left-right in the second round.

I didn't mean to start talking obstacles, hooks,
comebacks.
But, suddenly, I'm going down, saying:

I've been holding on with my teeth.
I've developed this strange social stutter.

I had to let my cutman go.

Fishing the Dream

MIKE DELP

1.   Half asleep
my hand begins to itch
where, hours ago,
I washed the blood from a brook trout
into the river,
and going into the dream,
I felt my hand arc,
tear away,
then circle back,
just above my line of sight,
waiting,
the great fins moving,
the eyes turned slate grey.
This was the beginning of waiting,
imagining the violence of the strike,
the bed moving,
then, limping downstairs,
the house gone icy,
thousands of fishhooks
tangled in the walls.

2.   For a while I stand on one leg
in the current,
letting the other trail off
in front of me,
imagine that it rips away,
then bobs to the surface downstream,
the toes pointed upward,
the calf muscles tight and blue
in the cold water.
In the dream I hobble after it,
and at the pool below Gould's Bend

I watch it glow in the bottom,
the tiny shreds of skin around the edges
waving back in forth in the movement of the river.
For a moment I want to dive down,
pick the stump up in my arms,
bring it to the bank
and try to put it back,
align it bone for bone,
then begin fishing again,
the smell of marrow on my fingers,
my hands holding the line, the rod,
fishing as if my life depended on it.

3.   It comes over and over:
I throw my line out
through the half-mist
hanging like a second skin
over the water,
but it doesn't stop,
just keeps going,
off into the air.
Moments pass,
then minutes.
Nothing.
I poke my rod toward the wall of fog,
hoping for something out there
to take hold,
but it passes through, into nothing.
For an hour I fish the dream,
never sure where my body stops
and the molecules of fog begin.
I sit down on the bank,
try to carve enough space
for my body,
then fold myself into my knees,

knowing that the line is still out there
the hook dragging the stillness.

4. In 1948, the year I was born,
    my father rescued Stan Ash
    from the Two-Hearted River
    by throwing a monofilament line over him,
    waited for his hand to catch,
    the line to burrow in
    and disappear under the flesh.
    Last night I felt that line
    cutting into my dream hand,
    and when my father pulled me to the surface
    the river suddenly widened,
    he seemed miles away.

    I sat up straight in bed,
    ran my finger down through the groove
    of my lifeline,
    felt the tug of the dream again,
    one hand circling in the air,
    my father on the bank,
    trying to bring me in
    so he could cut me free.

For the Death of Vince Lombardi

JAMES DICKEY

I never played for you. You'd have thrown
Me off the team on my best day —
No guts, maybe   not enough speed,
Yet running in my mind
As Paul Hornung, I made it here
With the others, sprinting down railroad tracks,
Hurdling bushes and backyard Cyclone
Fences, through city after city, to stand, at last, around you,
Exhausted, exalted, pale
As though you'd said "Nice going": pale
As a hospital wall. You are holding us
Millions together: those who played for you,
And those who entered the bodies
Of Bart Starr, Donny Anderson, Ray Nitschke, Jerry Kramer
Through the snowing tube on Sunday afternoon,
Warm, playing painlessly
In the snows of Green Bay Stadium, some of us drunk
On much-advertised beer   some old   some in other
Hospitals — most, middle-aged
And at home. Here you summon us, lying under
The surgical snows. Coach, look up: we are here:
We are held in this room
Like cancer.
The Crab has you, and to him
And to us you whisper
Drive, *Drive*. Jerry Kramer's face floats near — real, pale —
We others dream ourselves
Around you, and far away in the mountains, driving hard
Through the drifts, Marshall of the Vikings, plunging, burning
Twenty-dollar bills to stay alive, says, still
Alive, "I wouldn't be here
If it weren't for the lessons of football." Vince, they've told us;

When the surgeons got themselves
Together and cut loose
Two feet of your large intestine,
The Crab whirled up,   whirled out
Of the lost gut and caught you again
Higher up. Everyone's helpless
But cancer. Around your bed
The knocked-out teeth like hail-pebbles
Rattle down miles of adhesive tape from hands and ankles
Writhe in the room like vines   gallons of sweat
Blaze in buckets
In the corners   the blue and yellow of bruises
Make one vast sunset around you. No one understands you.
Coach, don't you know that some of us were ruined
For life? Everybody can't win. What of almost all
of us, Vince? We lost.
And our greatest loss was that we could not survive
Football. Paul Hornung has withdrawn
From me, and I am middle-aged and gray like these others.
What holds us here?
It is that you are dying by the code you made us
What we are by? Yes, Coach, it is true: love-hate is stronger
Than either love or hate. Into the weekly, inescapable dance
Of speed, deception, and pain
You led us, and brought us here weeping,
But as men. Or, you who created us as George
Patton created armies, did you discover the worst
In us: aggression, meanness, deception, delight in giving
Pain to others, for money? Did you make of us, indeed,
Figments   overspecialized, brutal ghosts
Who could have been real
Men in a better sense? Have you driven us mad
Over nothing? Does your death set us free?

Too late. We stand here among
Discarded TV commercials:
Among beer cans and razor blades and hair-tonic bottles,
Stinking with male deodorants: we stand here
Among teeth and filthy miles
Of unwound tapes, novocaine needles, contracts, champagne
Mixed with shower water,
Unraveling elastic, bloody face guards,
And the Crab, in his new, high position
Works soundlessly. In dying
You give us no choice, Coach,
Either. We've got to believe there's such a thing
As winning. The Sunday spirit-screen
Comes on   the bruise-colors brighten   deepen
On the wall   the last tooth spits itself free
Of a linebacker's aging head   knee cartilage cracks,
A boy wraps his face in a red jersey and crams it into
A rusty locker to sob, and we're with you
We're with you all the way
You're going forever, Vince.

The Death of the Race Car Driver

NORMAN DUBIE

I have not slept for a week.

It is matchless — this feeling
I have for the dream:

Baled hay burning in the air
With splintering planks of the barricade.
As I roll
I feel all over me, the silk drapery
Of boney French schoolgirls.

In the last month of the war,
Visiting a friend, I watched
A young nurse
Stare mindlessly past me
While soaping the testicles
Of an unconscious amputee . . .

At a hundred and eighty miles per hour
There's a little vibration in the chassis, a clarity
Like the musical waterglass
Gently tapped, but, here, silent and empty —
Speed and sleep have overlapped. My body,

Sack for eternity.

Competition

STEPHEN DUNN

Because he played games seriously
    and therefore knew grace
comes hard, rises through the cheap

in us, the petty, the entire history
    of our defeats,
he looked for grace in his opponents,

found a few friends that way
    and so many others
he could never drink with, talk to.

He learned early never to let up,
    never to give
a weaker opponent a gift

because so many times he'd been
    that person
and knew the humiliation in it,

being pandered to, a bone for the sad
    dog.
And because he remembered those times

after a loss when he'd failed
    at grace —
stole from the victor

the pleasures of pure victory
    by speaking
about a small injury or the cold

he wasn't quite over — he loved
   those opponents
who'd shake hands and give credit,

save their true and bitter stories
   for their lovers, later,
when all such lamentations are comic,

the sincere *if onlys* of grown men
   in short pants.
Oh there were people who thought

all of it so childish; what to say
   to them, how to agree,
ever, about dignity and fairness?

Nancy makes
Smth hard look easy

Criminal

STEPHEN DUNN

After Tonya & Nancy

Tonya
Harding
+
Nancy
Kerrigan

One woman has nothing out of place   A1
as she slides into our living rooms.   B
The other can't control her face,   A2

the past is in it, and something cheap insists   A
on the wrong, expensive gowns.   B
Unnerving, though: nothing out of place.   A1

Villanelle
19 lines
5 tercets
1 quatrain

We know no one is quite that chaste;   A
always near the palace are the ruins.   B
The other can't control her face,   A2

yet it's so hard for us to embrace   A
her, even broken-laced and fallen.   B
One woman has nothing out of place   A1

and, more unfair, she's all art and excellence.   A
Turn away, egalitarians.   B
The other who never learned to control her face   A2

applauds politely, smiles; what grace   A
she's willed only lasts seconds.   B
One is beautiful, has nothing out of place.   A1
The other can't control her face.   A2

Day and Night Handball

STEPHEN DUNN

I think of corner shots, the ball
hitting and dying like a butterfly
on a windshield, shots so fine
and perverse they begin to live

alongside weekends of sex
in your memory. I think of serves
delivered deep to the left hand,
the ball sliding off the side wall

into the blindnesses of one's body,
and diving returns that are impossible
except on days when your body is all
rubber bands and dreams

unfulfilled since childhood.
I think of a hand slicing the face
of a ball, so much english
that it comes back drunk

to your opponent who doesn't have
enough hands to hit it,
who hits it anyway, who makes you think
of "God!" and "Goddamn!," the pleasure

of falling to your knees
for what is superb, better than you.
But it's position I think of most,
the easy slam and victory

because you have a sense of yourself
and the court, the sense that old men
gone in the knees have,
one step in place of five,

finesse in place of power,
and all the time
the four walls around you
creating the hardship, the infinite variety.

Jack Johnson Does the Eagle Rock

CORNELIUS EADY

Perhaps he left the newspaper stand that morning
    dazed, a few pennies lighter,
The illustration of the crippled ocean liner
    with the berth he had the money
But not the skin to buy
Engraving itself
On that portion of the mind reserved for
    lucky breaks.
Perhaps the newsboy, a figure too small to
    bring back,
Actually heard his laugh,
As the *S.S. Titanic*, sans one prize fighter,
Goes down again all over New York,
Watched his body dance
As his arms lift the ship, now a simple millimeter thick,
    above his head
In the bustling air, lift it up
As though it was meant to happen.

Bullhead

JOHN ENGELS

Sprawled belly-down on the damp planks,
the breath squeezed in my chest,
I drift the worm into the pale
moon-shadow of the dock

and wait for the blunt emergence
of bullhead, his slow
surge to the bait, glint
of the small, mucusoid eye —
sluggish black spasm of flesh,

he bites, and I haul him out,
but he does not die at once.
Ugly among fishes, poisonous dorsal spine erect,
he endures, he swims in the air
for hours, scrabbles and grunts
in the bucket. A thousand times I've heard

that gross croak from the bucket.
Now it comes to memory from that peculiar sleeplessness
which loves those things which resemble

other things. Night after night
I have tried to breathe
the inappropriate air, wanted to cry out
into the blackness beyond
the dumb, immediate blackness

that I am about to die and cannot die,
but have made so dull a voice of the dull
connatural agony, I've writhed to it,
grunting aloud, the hook

of the breath snagged
in my gullet, the tongue
in my mouth like a worm.

The Man Who Beat Hemingway

MARTÍN ESPADA

for Kermit Forbes, Key West, Florida, 1994

In 1937, Robert Johnson
still sang the Walking Blues,
the insistent churchbell of his guitar,
the moaning congregation of his voice,
a year before the strychnine flavored
his whiskey.

In the time of Robert Johnson,
you called yourself Battling Geech,
135 pounds, the ball of your bicep rolling
when you sickled the left hook
from a crouch, elbows blocking
hammers to the ribcage.
Florida for a Black man
was Robert Johnson, moaning:
the signs that would not feed you
hand-lettered in diner windows,
the motels that kept all beds white.

Here, in a ring rigged behind the mansion,
next to the first swimming pool
in Key West, you sparred with Hemingway.
He was 260 pounds in 1937, thick arms
lunging for you, so you slid crablike
beneath him, your shaven head
spotlit with sweat against his chest.
Only once did his leather fist tumble you,
sprawling across canvas
white as sun.

Now, nearing eighty, one eye stolen
from the socket, one gold tooth
anchored to your jaw,
you awoke this morning
and weighed the hurricane-heavy air
of Key West in your fighter's hands,
three decades after Papa Hemingway
choked himself with a shotgun.
You should stand before the mansion
on Whitehead Street, telling the amazed tourists
that you are the man who beat Hemingway,
and it happened here,
even if the plaque
leaves out your name.

Pole Vaulter

DAVID ALLAN EVANS

The approach to the bar
is everything

unless I have counted
my steps   hit my markers
feel up to it   I refuse
to follow through
I am committed to beginnings
or to nothing

planting the pole
at runway's end
jolts me to my task
out of sprinting
I take off   kicking in
and up   my whole weight
trying the frailty
of fiberglass

never forcing myself
trusting it is right
to be taken to the end
of tension   poised for
the powerful thrust to
fly me beyond expectation

near the peak
I roll my thighs inward
arch my back   clearing
as much of the bar as I can
(knowing the best jump
can be cancelled
by a careless elbow)

and open my hands

Song of Racquetball

DAVID ALLAN EVANS

*Both in and out of the game and watching
and wondering about it.*
– Walt Whitman

1. I celebrate racquetball and sing racquetball,
   And what I shall assume you shall assume,
   For every breath belonging to me as good
         belongs to you.
   I celebrate passing shots, ceiling shots that skid
         and sizzle on the wall;
   I celebrate garbage serves, around-the-world shots.
   I find I incorporate roll-outs and drive serves,
         and am stucco'd with tie-breakers.
   And I say that a flat roll-out is no less than the
         journeywork of the stars,
   And a backhand fly-kill is miracle enough to
         stun the gods,
   And a man bending with lowered head to serve surpasses
         any statue.

2. I loaf and invite defeat,
   I advance forward when I should retreat backward,
   And am not contain'd between my headband and sneakers.
   My z-serve, my lob, every bead of sweat, every
         shot I know –
   I, now forty-seven years old in decent shape begin,
   Hoping to quit not till I drop dead on the court.

3. I am the poet of the backhand and I am the poet of
         the forehand,
   The pleasures of winning are with me and the pains of
         losing are with me.

I am the poet of the pinch shot the same as the fly-kill,
And I say there is nothing greater than an ace.
I scream the scream of self-hatred when I skip the ball,
We have had polite words long enough,
I show that swearing is part of the game.
Have you beaten the best? Are you Marty Hogan?
It is not important – surpass yourself.

I am he that feels the wet glove on my right hand, and
       the wet T-shirt and wristband,
I am he that fights for the center,
     loves the backhand lob serve,
     goes for the kill,
     aches with fatigue,
     stoops to pick up the ball,
I am he that craves time-outs, and the hearty handshakes
       of comrades.
I am he that needs a cold Budweiser.

4.   Who goes there, who steps into the court?
Dave Evans, Sr., racquetball player and poet,
Husband, father of three, martial artist, union man,
Boss-hater, ex–running back, confident and shy,
Introspective, deferential, balding, full of self-love
And self-hatred, loud drinker, fair fighter,
Lover of doubles as well as singles,
Oversexed, democratic, selfish and altruistic, easy
And tough, honest, paranoid, gullible, suspicious,
Pocketless of a nickel, unpretentious, believer in
Hard work, taker of naps, stocky, well calved,
Creative and gloomy, a cosmos, from Sioux City, Iowa.

5.   I know I am robust,
I do not worry about my energy level,
I see that passing shots never apologize,

I reckon I hit the ball as hard as most when
        I am in my groove.
I play my own game, that is enough,
And if no other player is aware I stand content.
And if each and every player is aware I stand content.
One man is aware and that is me,
And whether I win today or next week or next year,
I can cheerfully take it now, or with equal cheerfulness
        I can wait.
My sneakers are from Penney's,
I laugh at what you call skips,
And I know how to count to fifteen.

6. The lob serve swoops by and accuses me,
    It complains of my laziness,
    I sound my barbaric obscenity with rais'd racquet,
    I bequeath myself to runner-up trophies,
    If you want me, call 692-5214.

    You will hardly know who I am or what I am up to,
    But I shall be a worthy opponent,
    And give you a good sweat.

    Failing to beat me one day,
    Try again.
    I sit here close to the phone, waiting for you.

Body and Soul

B. H. FAIRCHILD

Half-numb, guzzling bourbon and Coke from coffee mugs,
our fathers fall in love with their own stories, nuzzling
the facts but mauling the truth, and my friend's father begins
to lay out with the slow ease of a blues ballad a story
about sandlot baseball in Commerce, Oklahoma, decades ago.
These were men's teams, grown men, some in their thirties
and forties who worked together in zinc mines or on oil rigs,
sweat and khaki and long beers after work, steel guitar music
whanging in their ears, little white rent houses to return to
where their wives complained about money and broken Kenmores
and then said the hell with it and sang *Body and Soul*
in the bathtub and later that evening with the kids asleep
lay in bed stroking their husband's wrist tattoo and smoking
Chesterfields from a fresh pack until everything was O.K.
Well, you get the idea. Life goes on, the next day is Sunday,
another ball game, and the other team shows up one man short.

They say, we're one man short, but can we use this boy,
he's only fifteen years old, and at least he'll make a game.
They take a look at the kid, muscular and kind of knowing
the way he holds his glove, with the shoulders loose,
the thick neck, but then with that boy's face under
a clump of angelic blonde hair, and say, oh, hell, sure,
let's play ball. So it all begins, the men loosening up,
joking about the fat catcher's sex life, it's so bad
last night he had to hump his wife, that sort of thing,
pairing off into little games of catch that heat up into
throwing matches, the smack of the fungo bat, lazy jogging
into right field, big smiles and arcs of tobacco juice,
and the talk that gives a cool, easy feeling to the air,
talk among men normally silent, normally brittle and a little
angry with the empty promise of their lives. But they chatter

74

and say rock and fire, babe, easy out, and go right ahead
and pitch to the boy, but nothing fancy, just hard fastballs
right around the belt, and the kid takes the first two
but on the third pops the bat around so quick and sure
that they pause a moment before turning around to watch
the ball still rising and finally dropping far beyond
the abandoned tractor that marks left field. Holy shit.
They're pretty quiet watching him round the bases,
but then, what the hell, the kid knows how to hit a ball,
so what, let's play some goddamned baseball here.
And so it goes. The next time up, the boy gets a look
at a very nifty low curve, then a slider, and the next one
is the curve again, and he sends it over the Allis Chalmers,
high and big and sweet. The left fielder just stands there, frozen.
As if this isn't enough, the next time up he bats left-handed.
They can't believe it, and the pitcher, a tall, mean-faced
man from Okarche who just doesn't give a shit anyway
because his wife ran off two years ago leaving him with
three little ones and a rusted-out Dodge with a cracked block,
leans in hard, looking at the fat catcher like he was the sonofabitch
who ran off with his wife, leans in and throws something
out of the dark, green hell of forbidden fastballs, something
that comes in at the knees and then leaps viciously towards
the kid's elbow. He swings exactly the way he did right-handed,
and they all turn like a chorus line toward deep right field
where the ball loses itself in sagebrush and the sad burnt
dust of dustbowl Oklahoma. It is something to see.

But why make a long story long: runs pile up on both sides,
the boy comes around five times, and five times the pitcher
is cursing both God and His mother as his chew of tobacco sours
into something resembling horse piss, and a ragged and bruised
Spalding baseball disappears into the far horizon. Goodnight,
Irene. They have lost the game and some painful side bets
and they have been suckered. And it means nothing to them
though it should to you when they are told the boy's name is

Mickey Mantle. And that's the story, and those are the facts.
But the facts are not the truth. I think, though, as I scan
the faces of these old men now lost in the innings of their youth,
I think I know what the truth of this story is, and I imagine
it lying there in the weeds behind that Allis Chalmers
just waiting for the obvious question to be asked: why, oh
why in hell didn't they just throw around the kid, walk him,
after he hit the third homer? Anybody would have,
especially nine men with disappointed wives and dirty socks
and diminishing expectations for whom winning at anything
meant everything. Men who knew how to play the game,
who had talent when the other team had nothing except this ringer
who without a pitch to hit was meaningless, and they could go home
with their little two-dollar side bets and stride into the house
singing *If You've Got the Money, Honey, I've Got the Time*
with a bottle of Southern Comfort under their arms and grab
Dixie or May Ella up and dance across the gray linoleum
as if it were V-Day all over again. But they did not.
And they did not because they were men, and this was a boy.
And they did not because sometimes after making love,
after smoking their Chesterfields in the cool silence and
listening to the big bands on the radio that sounded so glamorous,
so distant, they glanced over at their wives and noticed the lines
growing heavier around the eyes and mouth, felt what their wives
felt: that Les Brown and Glenn Miller and all those dancing couples
and in fact all possibility of human gaiety and light-heartedness
were as far away and unreachable as Times Square or the Avalon
ballroom. They did not because of the gray linoleum lying there
in the half-dark, the free calendar from the local mortuary
that said one day was pretty much like another, the work gloves
looped over the doorknob like dead squirrels. And they did not
because they had gone through a depression and a war that had left
them with the idea that being a man in the eyes of their fathers
and everyone else had cost them just too goddamned much to lay it
at the feet of a fifteen year-old boy. And so they did not walk him,
and lost, but at least had some ragged remnant of themselves

to take back home. But there is one thing more, though it is not
a fact. When I see my friend's father staring hard into the bottomless
well of home plate as Mantle's fifth homer heads toward Arkansas,
I know that this man with the half-orphaned children and
worthless Dodge has also encountered for his first and possibly
only time the vast gap between talent and genius, has seen
as few have in the harsh light of an Oklahoma Sunday, the blonde
and blue-eyed bringer of truth, who will not easily be forgiven.

Old Men Playing Basketball

B. H. FAIRCHILD

The heavy bodies lunge, the broken language
of fake and drive, glamorous jump shot
slowed to a stutter. Their gestures, in love
again with the pure geometry of curves,

rise toward the ball, falter, and fall away.
On the boards their hands and fingertips
tremble in tense little prayers of reach
and balance. Then, the grind of bone

and socket, the caught breath, the sigh,
the grunt of the body laboring to give
birth to itself. In their toiling and grand
sweeps, I wonder, do they still make love

to their wives, kissing the undersides
of their wrists, dancing the old soft-shoe
of desire? And on the long walk home
from the VFW, do they still sing

to the drunken moon? Stands full, clock
moving, the one in army fatigues
and houseshoes says to himself, *pick and roll,*
and the phrase sounds musical as ever,

radio crooning songs of love after the game,
the girl leaning back in the Chevy's front seat
as her raven hair flames in the shuddering
light of the outdoor movie, and now he drives,

gliding toward the net. A glass wand
of autumn light breaks over the backboard.
Boys rise up in old men, wings begin to sprout
at their backs. The ball turns in the darkening air.

Baseball Canto

LAWRENCE FERLINGHETTI

Watching baseball
sitting in the sun
eating popcorn
reading Ezra Pound

and wishing Juan Marichal
would hit a hole right through
the Anglo-Saxon tradition
in the First Canto
and demolish the barbarian invaders

When the San Francisco Giants take the field
and everybody stands up to the National Anthem
with some Irish tenor's voice
piped over the loudspeakers
with all the players struck dead in their places
and the white umpires like Irish cops
in their black suits and little black caps
pressed over their hearts
standing straight and still
like at some funeral of a blarney bartender
and all facing East
as if expecting some Great White Hope
or the Founding Fathers
to appear on the horizon
like 1066 or 1776 or all that

But Willie Mays appears instead
in the bottom of the first
and a roar goes up
  as he clouts the first one into the sun
    and takes off
      like a footrunner from Thebes

The ball is lost in the sun
    and maidens wail after him
        but he keeps running
            through the Anglo-Saxon epic

And Tito Fuentes comes up
    looking like a bullfighter
    in his tight pants and small pointed shoes

And the rightfield bleachers go mad
    with chicanos & blacks & Brooklyn beerdrinkers
        "Sweet Tito! Sock it to heem, Sweet Tito!"
And Sweet Tito puts his foot in the bucket
    and smacks one that don't come back at all
    and flees around the bases
like he's escaping from the United Fruit Company
    as the gringo dollar beats out the Pound
      and Sweet Tito beats it out
      like he's beating out usury
      not to mention fascism and anti-semitism

And Juan Marichal comes up
  and the chicano bleachers go loco again
    as Juan belts the first fast ball
      out of sight
        and rounds first and keeps going
    and rounds second and rounds third
      and keeps going
      and hits pay-dirt
    to the roars of the grungy populace
As some nut presses the backstage panic button
for the tape-recorded National Anthem again
to save the situation

but it don't stop nobody this time
in their revolution round the loaded white bases
in this last of the great Anglo-Saxon epics
in the *Territorio Libre* of baseball

Class A, Salem, the Rookie League

GARY FINCKE

We were drinking for free, bumming beers
From the past-their-prime by claiming
Ourselves Pittsburgh prospects, fireballers
Who'd broken in, last summer, at Salem.
We'd gotten a look in Columbus,
Three innings each in a courtesy game.
"Candelaria," we said, taking
Refills. What a party he threw
When the Pirates called him up that night.

We settled for Iron City, draft mugs.
It was semester break, sophomore year.
In three weeks, pitchers like us were due
In Bradenton, Florida, to prove
Ourselves for Double or Triple A,
And we wouldn't come back to this bar
At Easter unless the two of us
Were released, disabled, or home
For a sudden death in the family.

We said my mother was sick, my friend
Had a tender arm. We said we'd leave
Tickets for this tavern if either
Of us made Three Rivers, and drank four nights,
Underage, with men who supported us
Like fathers. They wanted names, who
To expect from Salem in three years,
The vets we'd met on their falls to sandlots,
Factories, or bars like Emerico's
Where they'd name, in turn, Al Oliver,
Dock Ellis, or the Steve Blass Syndrome,
Cite the strange, sad case of his lost control.

We were twenty miles from our old school,
Two districts from any fans we knew,
But there, one midnight, sat Mrs. Cook
Giving us her speech-class, critical look.
She could have offered *slower, louder,*
Breath control. She could have recited
A role call of our gradebook names, summoned
Us to the front of a fist-filled room
With the forensic demand for truth.

Glazed-green, the bar's surface suggested
Sea stories where the careless drown
In a tangle of cramps. We carried
A beer to her booth like homework;
One of the men who loved baseball
Slid in beside her. "From the Pirates,"
We said, trying to enunciate
Like athletes, setting our last story
Deep as we could in the farm system.

Pitcher

ROBERT FRANCIS

His art is eccentricity, his aim
How not to hit the mark he seems to aim at,

His passion how to avoid the obvious,
His technique how to vary the avoidance.

The others throw to be comprehended. He
Throws to be a moment misunderstood.

Yet not too much. Not errant, arrant, wild,
But every seeming aberration willed.

Not to, yet still, still to communicate
Making the batter understand too late.

The Rock Climbers

ROBERT FRANCIS

In this soft age, in my soft
middle age, the rock climbers

Who giving all to love
embrace cold cliffs

Or with spread-eagle arms
enact a crucifixion

Hanging between the falling
and the not-attaining

Observed or unobserved
by hawks and vultures —

How vaulting a humility
superb a supererogation

Craggy to break the mind
on and to cool the mind.

Two Wrestlers

ROBERT FRANCIS

Two bronzes, but they were passing bronze before
The sculptor

All glint, all gleaming, face to face and grace
To grace

Balanced almost beyond their balance, tingling
To spring —

Who ever saw so point-by-point, so perfect
A pair

That either one — or both — or neither one —
Could win?

If this is trickery, the trick is smooth
In truth

One wrestler challenging — oh how unsafe —
Himself.

Custom

CAROL FROST

As if it had forgotten everything — hatred, vindictiveness, the meaning
   of pain —
the bull took the ribboned sticks in his back without response, turning
   away,
so that when the picador entered the ring, the crowd was making fun
of the country's breeders. If there was an ounce of dignity or strength in
   the animal,
the picador would have to find it with his pole, and he came on slowly
to probe the back and shoulders:— deeply, cruelly, like a king with a
   scepter.
The bull barely moved until the picador gambled all and sailed his
   beautiful hat into the air
above the lowered head. With that the bull's will broke and he rushed
   again and again
like a child, a superbly angry prince, at the horse's side. When it was
   over, the bull
and its retinue gone inside to the abattoir, the picador, as was the cus-
   tom, reentered the ring.
The assembly roared — by his actions they knew they knew better who
   they were.

To Kill a Deer

CAROL FROST

Into the changes of autumn brush
the doe walked, and the hide, head and ears
were the tinsel browns. They made her.
I could not see her. She reappeared, stuffed with apples,
and I shot her. Into the pines she ran,
and I ran after. I might have lost her,
seeing no sign of blood or scuffle,
but felt myself part of the woods,
a woman with a doe's ears, and heard her
dying, counted her last breaths like a song
of dying, and found her dying.
I shot her again because her eyes
were open, and her lungs rattled like castanets,
then poked her with the gun barrel
because her eyes were dusty and unreal.
I opened her belly and pushed the insides
like rotted fruit into a rabbit hole,
skinned her, broke her leg joints under my knee,
took the meat, smelled the half-digested smell
that was herself. Ah, I closed her eyes.
I left her refolded in some briars
with the last sun on her head
like a benediction head tilted on its axis
of neck and barren bone; head bent
wordless over a death, though I heard
the night wind blowing through her fur,
heard riot in the emptied head.

The Knot Hole Gang

BRENDAN GALVIN

DeMarco said the special bus
from Braves' Field would pick us up
at a park way across town, a red bus
with an Indian's head on the front
just like the one on the nickel
it took to admit us to the bleachers,
and he led the way
to a mange of dust and grass
an hour from home, named for a war hero,
with its swings knotted irrevocably
and one kid who stayed
behind the chain link fence and said,
"Hey kid, it ain't gonna come,"
over and over till Marchant
chased him with a bat.
Somebody shouted "Here it comes!"
every time a truck
backfired out on the parkway,
and if you had driven by on your way
to the track and seen us there,
you might have thought how American
we were in our baseball caps,
with gloves the size of bushel baskets
on our belts, their palms thumped
black, with smiles torn out
at our knees and our ankles bulging
the rubber discs on those Keds
that each spring made teachers throw
all the windows open and beg us
never to wear them to school again,
with our lunch bags sweating
sandwich oils through the long afternoon.

Running

BRENDAN GALVIN

Experts say for me to do it well
I should be forty pounds lighter
or twenty-one inches taller,

so if I do it I'm a fool,
fat fool if I don't.
Dying of experts, I shuck off

home by the back door,
taking myself to yappers at heels
and the nameless worst who may

break anywhere from bushes,
my mind holding its hand,
telling itself the teeth of the unknown

dissolve when confronted even in fear.
If you see me and toot, I may have
only my middle finger for you:

I'm not sponsored by the National
Park Service for your viewing pleasure,
have had shin splints, and suffer

permanently from Morton's Foot.
Experts say any moment my spine
may collapse from cervix to coccyx.

But look, there is heavy traffic of bees
in the burst willow catkins, that kingfisher
dips and rises over the marsh

like a lesson in scansion.
A month from here, swallows will loop and dive,
slicing the air close to my doubling heartbeat,

two months and a woodcock
will sail through a steep
parabola ending in bushes.

I let a fly live completely a moment
in the dampening bush of my hair.
Rhythms are breaking, the last shred of

human song just flew out of my head.
Once I awaited adrenalin's uppercut under
my limping heart, and paused like

a man in mid-celebration
recalled to final things. Red fish
school up in the blood. Whatever I need,

there's no name for it, but we are
a naturally healthy people,
being of the Elect, so this must be

somehow un-American. Any minute now,
Flab will dust me off with his Pontiac,
but here on the edge of energy

I believe even the stumps will fly again.
What expert ever saw a hawk go before him
toward a quarter moon pale in the western sky,

or a random butterfly exploring the air
over bayberries? All things are pilgrims,
except maybe the blacksnake soaking up

asphalt's watery heat, who is only inertia
to be overcome. Shifts change in the blood,
but I'm breaking no records. By mile four

I'm only framework a breeze passes through.
Bellies of gulls on the flats
are lit like quarts of milk. This wobbling

under my ribs dessicates bad habits.
I slow to a trot, to the least piper's
whistling, and my pulse begins its

shorebird glossolalia. It says
dowitcher coot yellowlegs
brant bufflehead knot

Shadow-Casting

JAMES GALVIN

This boy's father dies.

Fine.

It always happens.

The boy knows
what to do.

He goes fishing the same stretch of water he angled
with his father all his life till now.

The beaver ponds shine
like a string of pearls.

It isn't easy to fly-cast a mirror-
finish.

The ponds are silting in.

It always happens.

They turn
into meadows.

The stream is choked with sweet-smelling grasses,
cottonwoods, and willows.

He knows what to do with fifty feet
of line out, shadow-casting.

The loops flash over his head, electric
in the sunlight, as if to illustrate grief, or the hem of a luminous
dress in motion.

Then the tapered line rifles out, and the lead-
wing touches water with no more force than its own tiny weight.

The surface breaks.

They call them rainbows for a reason.

The boy
opens his father's clasp-knife to open the fish.

As he does this some lint trapped under the blade, like a cottonwood seed from his father's pocket, falls out and parachutes down to the grass, and suddenly this boy, it always happens, doesn't know what to do anymore.

4th Base

GARY GILDNER

Decked out in flannels and gripping my mitt
I was running laps, long grassy laps,
and hearing my 200 bones start to chatter –
I had finally arrived in the major leagues!

I stopped in the infield, dropping
to a shoulder stand – my big toes pointing out the sun! –
and there was no pain, even at 37.

Then we started to play – I was at 4th –
and my first throw over to 1st
bounced in on the 10th or 11th dribble.

Odd, I thought,
that the game had developed such wrinkles.
But shuck that, I was here now, bounding
around my sack like a well-oiled seal, barking
"Dust everyone off! Dust everyone off!"

After a while I slipped into Mass
and sat with my old teammates –
the ones from high school who had grown pink
and jowly, and who played with their keys
between their knees, and who
when the choir leaned forward to sing our song
covered their eyes, and mumbled, and wouldn't look at me.

The Racer's Widow

LOUISE GLÜCK

The elements have merged into solicitude,
Spasms of violets rise above the mud
And weed, and soon the birds and ancients
Will be starting to arrive, bereaving points
South. But never mind. It is not painful to discuss
His death. I have been primed for this —
For separation — for so long. But still his face assaults
Me; I can hear that car careen again, the crowd coagulate on
 asphalt
In my sleep. And watching him, I feel my legs like snow
That let him finally let him go
As he lies draining there. And see
How even he did not get to keep that lovely body.

Line Drive Caught by the Grace of God

LINDA GREGERSON

Half of America doubtless has the whole
of the infield's peculiar heroics by heart,
this one's way with a fractured forearm,
that one with women and off-season brawls,

the ones who are down to business while their owner
goes to the press. You know them already, the quaint
tight pants, the heft
and repose and adroitness of men

who are kept for a while while they age
with the game. It's time
that parses the other fields too,
one time you squander, next time you hoard,

while around the diamond summer runs
its mortal stall, the torso that thickens,
the face that dismantles its uniform.
And sometimes pure felicity, the length

of a player suspended above the dirt
for a wholly deliberate, perfect catch
for nothing, for New York,
for a million-dollar contract which is nothing now,

for free, for the body
as it plays its deft decline and countless humbling,
deadly jokes, so the body
may once have flattered our purposes.

A man like you or me but for this moment's
delay and the grace of God. My neighbor
goes hungry when the Yankees lose,
his wife's too unhappy to cook,

but supper's a small enough price to pay,
he'd tell you himself, for odds
that make the weeks go by so personal,
so hand in glove.

Skateboard

THOM GUNN

Tow Head on his skateboard
threads through a crowd
of feet and faces delayed
to a slow stupidity.
Darts, doubles, twists.
You notice how nimbly
the body itself has learned
to assess the relation between
the board, pedestrians,
and immediate sidewalk.
Emblem. Emblem of fashion.
Wearing dirty white
in dishevelment as delicate
as the falling draperies
on a dandyish
Renaissance saint.
Chain round his waist.
One hand gloved.
Hair dyed to show it is dyed,
pale flame spiking from fuel.
Tow Head on Skateboard
perfecting himself:
emblem extraordinary
of the ordinary.

In the sexless face
eyes innocent of feeling
therefore suggest the spirit.

The Fifth Inning

DONALD HALL

1.   Kurt, last night Dwight Evans put it all
together, the way you made collage,
with a ridiculous catch followed
by an assist at first base, a hit
in the seventh inning for the tie,
and another in the last of the
ninth to pull it out at Fenway Park,
and win the game. Madness and method
in "Baseball" gathers bits and pieces

2.   of ordinary things — like bleacher
ticket stubs, used Astroturf, Fenway
Frank wrappers, yearbooks, and memory —
to paste them onto the bonkers grid
of the page. I stood at the workbench
after school and all day on weekends
every day for months that seem decades
now — and I stand there still, in the dark
cellar on Ardmore Street, cutting and
gluing, my tongue protruding from my

3.   lips, and nothing flies. When my daughter —
bored at thirteen by the grownup talk
at the fancy picnic outside the
theater in Stratford, Ontario —
remarked frequently on the paddle
boats out on the lake ("Oh, look! . . ." "*That* looks
like fun! . . ." "I wonder where they start from?"),
I understood: I said, "Let's go find
the place they start from and rent a boat."

4. Her face livened up; but she was smart:
As we walked toward the pier together,
she asked: "Are you certain you want to
do this, or are you doing it just
to be mean?" In nineteen-thirty-eight,
the hurricane lifted Aunt Clara's
cottage at Silver Sands and carried
it twenty yards to deposit it
in a salt meadow; the tidal wave

5. overwhelmed the Thimble Island where
Uncle Arthur lived. When rain started
in the second inning at Fenway
Park, it drizzled on umbrellas raised
in boxes by the field. Most of us
climbed to remote seats back under the
overhang to watch the (I wrote this
before, back in the second inning)
puddles pocked by raindrops. In the lights

6. we made out straight up-and-down falling
pencil lines of rain that the pitchers
squinted through to see the catchers' signs;
batters peered to watch how the ball spun.
After six innings it rained harder
and the umpire suspended play – game
tied three to three – then called it an hour
later. We struggled wetly out from
a game without issue. The young men

7. partied and slept, to make tomorrow's
double header at five. All night I
slept and woke practicing – obsessive
even in sleep, just as I bully

notes into lines — how the slow rain fell
like time measured in vertical light.
When I was a child, Connecticut
in the thirties and forties, we drove
to Ebbets Field or the Polo Grounds,

8.   a couple of hours down the newly
constructed or incomplete parkways
to Brooklyn especially, dense with
its tiny park and passionate crowd.
After Billy Herman brilliantly
stopped a ground ball and flipped to Pee Wee
for the force, I turned immediate
attention to a vendor and my
father thought I missed the lucky play.

9.   While that was happening, Kurt, I guess
you left Germany for England. Good.
As I thought about Curt (sic) Davis,
you were building your Merz-apartment.
I watched the first game of the nineteen-
forty-one World Series in the Bronx,
when Joe Gordon took Curtsic Davis
deep; we lost three to two, unable
to rally back. Then the long drive home.

The Eighth Inning

DONALD HALL

1. Kurt, terror is merely the thesis:
   Ten years later the guerrilla chief
   swears himself in as President-for-
   Life, appointing Commando Plastique
   his Minister for Health and Welfare.
   Meanwhile former Emperor Pluto
   wags his tail at the Zurich Hilton,
   attended by his Secretary
   Miss Universe-*und*-Swiss-Bankaccount.

2. However, Kurt, we must inform you
   with regret (you will not be surprised)
   that The Committee of Reconcil-
   iation finds itself unable
   to attend the ceremonies, nor
   will it observe the Riviera
   reunion of the secret police:
   The peacemakers have been mouldering
   in their mass grave for a decade. I

3. cherish the photograph on my wall,
   Kurt, where you embrace Bambino Babe
   Ruth (Tokyo, nineteen-twenty-eight.)
   Photography's dolor is common:
   We are forever older than our
   photographs. Even a Polaroid —
   by the time the fish of the image
   has swum to the surface and settled
   into its fins and fortunes for all

4.   eternity — measures another
sixty seconds fading toward the grave.
Baseball like sexual intercourse
and art stops short, for a moment, the
indecent continual motion
of time forward implying our death
and imminent decomposition.
Did you ever marry the bottle?
I married Scotch when I was forty.

5.   For two years we kept house together.
She constructed pale renewable
joy like a summer twilight; she was
impassive, agreeable, faithful,
forgiving; was princess and dragon,
church and castle, Eden and Elm Street,
hell and heaven blended together.
If it were not God's will, the baseball
would disintegrate when the pitcher

6.   touched it. We say grace to implore that
our food remain among visible
things: Only His Will sustains carrots.
Flying over China we saw base-
ball diamonds in the sun. Guangzho and
Shenyang, the smallest of our cities,
each kept four million people. We walked
at night in the light from small shops, pale
anomalous tall phantoms with big

7.   noses in the grave polloi that roiled
multitudinousness everywhere.
In Chengdu at night the scroll-sellers
played flashlights over their wares — bamboo,
dragons, snapdragons — that hung from ropes
strung between poplars. In the full moon

the fox walks on snow, black prints of fox;
but the chicken's head has migrated
to the pigsty already. Oink. Oink.

8.   Baseball in the winter is our dream's
retrospective summer, and even
(d. v.) the summer of prospect, game
perfectly mental that we control
by the addition of our wishful
selves throwing, catching, hitting, running
bases, staring with the same eyes back
and forth as pitcher and as batter.
No game plays its theatre so nightly:

9.   It never rains on this Wrigley Field;
in this Tiger Stadium it is
always Ebbets Field, the Polo Grounds,
Forbes Field, Griffith Stadium, Braves Field,
and Comiskey Park. Whatever's green,
it's not grass; those aren't hot dogs either;
but when we depart the old within —
Fenway of January and snow,
we find ticket stubs in our wallets.

Allegiance

FORREST HAMER

I loved the Supremes as much as baseball
at eleven, my first base plate a stage.
So in those summertime lulls in action,
all base hits easily thwarted, I sang
the way Diana Ross did — rare and
heavy-lidded, often about some love
that did her wrong. The background girls concurred.
And I noticed myself changing pronouns,
suddenly aware that the other boys
listened closely to their first baseman,
more now than he had, reminding him
how necessary practice is with pronouns,
converting he to she at every turn;
otherwise a guy on the other team
might get past you, and then another one
could bat him in, the other side winning
and your whole team holding you responsible.

Archives

MICHAEL S. HARPER

Cooperstown, N.Y.

Photos and clippings fade;
no one can find a real signature
of Rube Foster, who put together
the Negro Leagues; efforts
at why Josh Gibson died at thirty-
five are even vaguer,
his sleek strong body in the waves
of San Juan the vintage year:
1934. Later, 72 home runs,
the only ball over the third tier
at Yankee Stadium
for the games on off-days.

No flicks of Gibson as a Globe-
trotter, his golden gloves
astride the mound captured,
for real, with Curt Flood,
eating steaks on a grill,
in a parking lot in spring
training. Reggie is a mask,
astride a roadster, a paltry
lid on a rainday with Vida Blue.

Frank Robinson's loaded automatic
put him under arrest; the flick
of his headrag, a white mop,
only shown in Cincinnati,
eating Satchel's 45-lb. catfish,
chasing "Willmont" Liquors, Inc.
as endorsements in Brooklyn.

The clippings of the rest
of Negro America are full of glee;
no ounce of bitterness,
except for Jackie, who hit
better than they thought,
and was fast, stealing home
in public, voting Republican,
the whole Civil War
on his back and pigeon-toes.

On PBS the documentaries,
one trailer sideshow,
a whole hall of oral history
in transcriptions
of black and white.

Trujillo, who paid the best,
threatened execution if you lost;
the black World Series in Comiskey
full of chicken, zoot suits,
trainfare from everywhere
but endorsements, turnstyles.

"Let's play two."

Homage to the Brown Bomber

MICHAEL S. HARPER

Speed of the punch,
its dancing, rhythmic fluency
in short space, short duration,
its honing light of the Garden,
the Stadium: each gladiator falls
to be redeemed in porcelain speech,
however simple, never glib,
the nation's devastation
coming home to roost.

Born near sacred Indian mounds in Alabama,
broken in the "destroy" kitchens
of Chevrolet and Cadillac,
short tours at Comiskey Park,
the heavy bag the strange fruit
of commerce, newsprint,
without the dazzling photographs
of Sonja Henie's pirouettes
at the Olympic Games,
in shared bedrooms, horns
plenty for the unprotected.

Sugar dazzled too,
but the brute poetry
of the finisher,
how to wait on hidden impulse
of a bannered song,
that was ammunition
for the lost struggle
of the chaingang,
of the limousine.

Taps at Vegas,
new shrubbery
at Arlington,
grist for radio, the stooped flares
of camels
on deserts of yesterdays,
bright lungs blanching tomorrows,
barrows at rest.

Makin' Jump Shots

MICHAEL S. HARPER

He waltzes into the lane
'cross the free-throw line,
fakes a drive, pivots,
floats from the asphalt turf
in an arc of black light,
and sinks two into the chains.

One on one he fakes
down the main, passes
into the free lane
and hits the chains.

A sniff in the fallen air —
he stuffs it through the chains
riding high:
"traveling" someone calls —
and he laughs, stepping
to a silent beat, gliding
as he sinks two into the chains.

Hitting Golfballs off the Bluff

JEFFREY HARRISON

They come back now, those nights my friend and I
hit golfballs off the bluff behind his house.
We were sixteen and had our learner's permits
but no girlfriends, unlike the football jocks
we couldn't stand but secretly envied.
Neither of us actually played golf,
but late one night we took his father's clubs
and started what became a ritual.
A Freudian would have a field day with it:
the clubs, the balls, the deep ravine below
with train tracks and a river running through it.
But for us it was pure exhilaration:
the sure feel of a good connection, zing
of the white ball disappearing into blackness,
then silence as we waited for the thud
against the ground below, splash in the river,
or bang against the roof of a freight car.
That drawn-out moment when we only listened,
holding our laughter back, seemed never-ending
and one time was: no sound came back at all,
as if we'd sent the golfball into orbit
like a new planet — one we might still see
moving across the sky on any night,
pocked like the moon, but smaller, shining green
with envy now, now deep red with desire.

Pool Is a Godless Sport

JAMES HAUG

I like the articulate crack
the cue ball makes
on impact, how it drops
what it's after and backspins back,
the chalk skids
on its bald surface, blue
and hard as water
or your eye, keen straight
down the line of the poolstick,
how the clogged air of lies
and smoke clears as you circle
the table, the next shot
plump on the rail, a duck.
You're on a roll, playing
collisions of intent and dumb luck.
We don't talk as I gather
a new game in the rack;
no one's put down quarters.
We could shoot hours here.
The bartender yawns and looks on,
pinball bangs a free ball.
We play off the angles, combinations,
the felt before each break
fresh as promise,
and let the rolling geometry
plot our next move.

The Diver

ROBERT HAYDEN

Sank through easeful
azure. Flower
creatures flashed and
shimmered there —
lost images
fadingly remembered.
Swiftly descended
into canyon of cold
nightgreen emptiness.
Freefalling, weightless
as in dreams of
wingless flight,
plunged through infra-
space and came to
the dead ship,
carcass that swarmed with
voracious life.
Angelfish, their
lively blue and
yellow prised from
darkness by the
flashlight's beam,
thronged her portholes.
Moss of bryozoans
blurred, obscured her
metal. Snappers,
gold groupers explored her,
fearless of bubbling
manfish. I entered
the wreck, awed by her silence,
feeling more keenly
the iron cold.

With flashlight probing
fogs of water
saw the sad slow
dance of gilded
chairs, the ectoplasmic
swirl of garments,
drowned instruments
of buoyancy,
drunken shoes. Then
livid gesturings,
eldritch hide and
seek of laughing
faces. I yearned to
find those hidden
ones, to fling aside
the mask and call to them,
yield to rapturous
whisperings, have
done with self and
every dinning
vain complexity.
Yet in languid
frenzy strove, as
one freezing fights off
sleep desiring sleep;
strove against the
cancelling arms that
suddenly surrounded
me, fled the numbing
kisses that I craved.
Reflex of life-wish?
Respirator's brittle
belling? Swam from
the ship somehow;
somehow began the
measured rise.

To the Man Saying "Come on Seis" at Hollywood Park

DAVID HAYWARD

All the great jockeys were born premature.
Willie Shoemaker spent his first nights in a shoebox incubator
in his grandmother's oven. He weighed two pounds,
and two years after retiring from the one job
in which an ambulance follows you as you work,
he was paralyzed in a car accident. Terrible

the little gussied-up bodies and terrible for anyone
to want a lawn jockey of his own, with no designs
on any oval, no horse even. At the Silk Hat
arcade in Tokyo, though, to project one's wishes
onto a tiny plastic white man,
of a piece with his horse and nodding

in his groove to the finish, is to see
the whole world, pylon and Creamsicle,
abbreviated in him. Bee Nun (who, like the other horses,
is all name) comes in at 40 to 1 and the slot gushes tokens
all the doo-dah day, a thousand gentleman
rabbits in coin, eager for use

but redeemable for other tokens only. A closed circuit,
then, unbeautiful as the system of condensation
and rain, with nothing left over, no blanket
of losing tickets over which to walk home, as this man
and I did, done with our words, "Come on *Seis*," "Five.
Oh Five. Five," which were not prayer but "I chose this."

When we both walked out empty-handed,
our money come to what it really was,
the world — a parking lot littered with wet,
unwanted souvenir clocks — looked to me
the way wreaths of red carnations
must look to the horse who's won them.

Mantle

WILLIAM HEYEN

Mantle ran so hard, they said,
he tore his legs to pieces.
What is this but spirit?

52 homers in '56, the triple crown.
I was a high school junior batting
fourth behind him in a dream.

I prayed for him to quit, before
his lifetime dropped below .300.
But he didn't, and it did.

He makes Brylcreem commercials now,
models with open mouths draped around him
as they never were in Commerce, Oklahoma,

where the sandy-haired, wide-shouldered boy
stood up against his barn,
lefty for an hour (Ruth, Gehrig),

then righty (DiMaggio),
as his father winged them in,
and the future blew toward him

now a fastball, now a slow
curve hanging
like a model's smile.

The Stadium

WILLIAM HEYEN

The stadium is filled,
for this is the third night the moon
has not appeared as even a thin sickle.

We light the candles we were told to bring.
The diamond is lit red with torches.
Children run the bases.

A voice, as though from a tomb,
leads us to the last amen of a hymn.
Whole sections of the bleachers begin to moan.

The clergy files from the dugout
to the makeshift communion rails
that line the infield grass.

We've known, all our lives,
that we would gather here in the stadium
on just such a night,

that even the bravest among us
would weep softly in the dark aisles,
catching their difficult breath.

Tennis in the City

FRANK HIGGINS

for Arthur Ashe

He could help us out
selling papers or sacking groceries
but that's what I did growing up.
Every day he's in the alley
knocking that ball against the building.
Whomp   take that   Forest Hills
whomp   whomp   take that   Wimbledon
whomp   whomp   whomp
all   day   long,
the wife tells me so.
Says she watches him from the window
when the bossman has her clean 'em,
says she doesn't know about that boy.
But I know about that boy
and I know this ball's worn
and I know this racket's gonna split
no matter how much tape you put on,
so tonight after supper
we're going for new ones, son.
And I want you to start staying
in that alley an hour longer, hear?

The Y

BRENDA HILLMAN

They are bringing back the bones of Che Guevara
    so the system of global capitalism
    will be reversed while a girl on the stairmaster
    reads *Anna Karenina*, pausing at the part
    where Vronsky, thinking Anna into the wrong coldness,
    might turn his back on her another time. The girl
    would name her dog for him if she had one. Legs with
    multiple tattoos of heavenly bodies — ceil-
    ing stars, comets, moons — push weights. The room shakes, and
        east of here,
    aspen forests growing from root systems that never
    die send out shoots above ground anyway because
    the lust to be individual exceeds the
    desire to lie down anonymously above
    a mantle of fire. No one's arguing about
    formal necessity or the power below
    survival or if they wanted to be touched, there.

I Try to Turn in My Jock

DAVID HILTON

The way I see it, is that when I step out on that court
and feel inside that I can't make the plays,
it'll be time to call it quits. – Elgin Baylor

Going up for the jump shot,
Giving the kid the head-fakes and all
'Til he's jocked right out the door of the gym
And I'm free at the top with the ball and my touch,
Lofting the arc off my fingertips,
I feel my left calf turn to stone
And my ankle warp inward to form when I land
A neat right angle with my leg,
And I'm on the floor,
A pile of sweat and sick muscles,
Saying,
Hilton,
You're 29, getting fat,
Can't drive to your right anymore,
You can think of better things to do
On Saturday afternoons than be a chump
For a bunch of sophomore third-stringers;
Join the Y, steam and martinis and muscletone.
But, shit,
The shot goes in.

Fast Break

EDWARD HIRSCH

In Memory of Dennis Turner, 1946–1984

A hook shot kisses the rim and
hangs there, helplessly, but doesn't drop

and for once our gangly starting center
boxes out his man and times his jump

perfectly, gathering the orange leather
from the air like a cherished possession

and spinning around to throw a strike
to the outlet who is already shoveling

an underhand pass toward the other guard
scissoring past a flat-footed defender

who looks stunned and nailed to the floor
in the wrong direction, turning to catch sight

of a high, gliding dribble and a man
letting the play develop in front of him

in slow motion, almost exactly
like a coach's drawing on the blackboard,

both forwards racing down the court
the way that forwards should, fanning out

and filling the lanes in tandem, moving
together as brothers passing the ball

between them without a dribble, without
a single bounce hitting the hardwood

until the guard finally lunges out
and commits to the wrong man

while the power-forward explodes past them
in a fury, taking the ball into the air

by himself now and laying it gently
against the glass for a layup,

but losing his balance in the process,
inexplicably falling, hitting the floor

with a wild, headlong motion
for the game he loved like a country

and swiveling back to see an orange blur
floating perfectly through the net.

How to Play Night Baseball

JONATHAN HOLDEN

A pasture is best, freshly
mown so that by the time a grounder's
plowed through all that chewed, spit-out
grass to reach you, the ball
will be bruised with green kisses. Start
in the evening. Come
with a bad sunburn and smelling of chlorine,
water still crackling in your ears.
Play until the ball is khaki —
a movable piece of the twilight —
the girls' bare arms in the bleachers are pale,
and heat lightning jumps in the west. Play
until you can only see pop-ups,
and routine grounders get lost in
the sweet grass for extra bases.

[Handwritten annotation:] No meter or rhyme scheme. Free verse

A Poem for Ed "Whitey" Ford

JONATHAN HOLDEN

I wanted my name
curt: Ed
Ford: a name that gave away
nothing. I wanted
a cute cocky face. To be
a low-ball specialist
but sneaky fast, tough
in the clutch. Not
to retire the side with power
but with finesse.
I never wanted to go
soft, to fall in love fall
through it and keep falling like this,
letting the light and air
pick my pockets at will.
Or dwell in this gray
area, this interval
where we search out by feel
the seams in the day,
homesick for the warm
map of a hand.
I planned to be
immune as Ford
on the throne of the mound,
my position defined
by both taut foul-lines,
the fence against my back.
To sight on the vanishing point
in the core of the mitt.
My delivery strict,
classic.

Not to sit thinking like this
how I drive the blunt wedge
of my breath before me
one space at a time,
watching words
I thought were well meant
miss. I wanted
what we all wanted then:
To be ice.
To throw uncontradicted
strikes. To be
like Ed Ford at work —
empty, cruel, accurate.
Our beauty pure expertise.

Baseball

PAUL HOOVER

When the world finally ends,
a baseball will be hovering
over a diamond somewhere in New Jersey:
a flash of flesh falling out of its clothes
and suddenly no one's there.
The baseball, singed and glowing,
drops to the ground again.
But let's back up twenty years or so.
It's the 1970s and the Oakland A's
have 19th Century faces,
as if they'd stepped from a Balzac novel
belatedly in spring.
A dynasty of troublesome players
who like to fight and slide,
they've just won their third World Series
but trip on their long hair
and wear Edwardian clothes,
the messy but dressy look.
Back then, I'd lie in bed all day,
watching the Cubs and Watergate
on a black and white TV.
Then I'd get up, write some poems,
and pick the goldfish off the floor,
which liked to leap from its tank
because the kissing gouramis
would suck pink holes in its sides.
The poems were not about kissing
but had a violent side,
the way a man's gaze can be "violent,"
fixing you into an object
that, while it lacks a "lack,"
stands up like a fetish.

You feel your face go rubber,
as if your body were filling
with grief. Meanwhile, Reggie Jackson,
while not completely phallocentric,
did create a firm impression
as he "stroked" the ball
for a homer. Sometimes
he flailed and fell, but now
he's out of ball. Left-handedness
is a sinister business, but in
the major leagues, you want
a few of these wizards
on first base or the mound.
Does "mound" have a sexual sound?
And what about "stick men"?
Baseball in the movies —
for instance *Field of Dreams* —
is basically conservative,
says Pauline Kael and one agrees:
"Play ball" is the message,
the dream of male tradition
passing and to come. Besides,
those uniforms, so quasi-pseudo-
semi-demi-military in fashion.
They make us watch them swing
their sticks, slide between
another man's legs, as if
that torso heaven were all
the spit we're worth, we who
sit and dream, eat and talk,
as gulls stir over the field.
I like to watch the grass,
a simple wedge of astonishment
each time I enter the park.
Then the boffo noise of the crowd
chucks and drones like an engine.

I want a hot dog now! And beer
to spill down concrete steps.
My goodness, some of those guys
actually look like gods!
And some of them look just
upwardly mobile, tossing a wink
at their accountants Horvath,
Perkins, Wiggins, and Peal.
One imagines the Yankee Clipper,
smooth as smoke, crossing an outfield of fog.
Lou Gehrig stands at the mike,
saying an iron goodbye, and Babe Ruth
points at the fence where the ball
will probably go if all the myths
were right. Here's Pepper Martin
putting his spikes in your face,
Dizzy Dean's elegant rasp
as he chews a point with Pee Wee Reese.
I remember when Cincinnati
had Birdie Tebbetts, Dusty Rhodes,
Vada Pinson, and Ted Kluszewski.
The sponsor was Hudepohl beer,
and they played in Crosley Field.
The man sitting next to us
waved a gun whenever a run was scored,
then put it back in his girlfriend's
purse. We thought that was fine.
Claes Oldenburg insists
baseball is an "aesthetic game,"
all that flutter of color
creating the eye when strict rows
randomly move. But "poetry in motion"?
I can't say I believe. Poetry
comes in your mouth like flesh;
it rises to the surface
like a ball held underwater,

bouncing a little but staying there,
hardly transcendental but present
nevertheless. You watch it watching you,
staying and going, the silk
suck of a curtain that seems
to leave the building by way
of a window one day, then slips
back over the sill because a door
was opened. Its absolute feet
aren't there, disappearing like
a corner the moment you approach.
Baseball, on the other hand,
presents itself like air,
love's green moment still,
at two in the afternoon.

From Altitude, the Diamonds

RICHARD HUGO

You can always spot them, even from high up,
the brown bulged out trying to make a circle
of a square, the green square inside the brown,
inside the green the brown circle you know is mound
and the big outside green rounded off by a round line
you know is fence. And no one playing.

You've played on every one. Second base somewhere
on the Dallas Tucson run, New Mexico you think,
where green was brown. Right field outside Chicago
where the fans went silent when you tripled home
the run that beat their best, their all-season
undefeated home town Sox. What a game you pitched
that hot day in the Bronx. You lost to that left hander,
Ford, who made it big, one-nothing on a fluke.
Who's to believe it now? Fat. Bald. Smoking your fear
of the turbulent air you are flying, remembering
the war, a worse fear, the jolting flak, the prayer.

When air settles, the white beneath you opens
and far below in some unpopulated region
of whatever state you are over (it can't be Idaho,
that was years ago) you spot a tiny diamond,
and because you've grown far sighted with age
you see players moving, the center fielder
running the ball down deep, two runners
rounding third, the third base coach waving hard
and the hitter on his own not slowing down
at second, his lungs filled with the cheers of those
he has loved forever, on his magnificent tiny way
to an easy stand-up three.

Letter to Mantsch from Havre

RICHARD HUGO

Dear Mike: We didn't have a chance. Our starter had no change
and second base had not been plugged since early in July.
How this town turned out opening night of the tournament
to watch their Valley Furniture team wipe us, the No-
Name Tavern of Missoula, out. Remember Monty Holden,
ace Havre pitcher, barber, hero of the Highline, and his
tricky "catch-this" windup? First inning, when you hit that shot,
one on, the stands went stone. It still rockets the night.
I imagine it climbing today, somewhere in the universe,
lovelier than a girl climbs on a horse and lovelier than star.
We lost that game. No matter. Won another. Lost again
and went back talking fondly of your four home runs,
triple and single in three games, glowing in the record book.
I came back after poems. They ask me today, here in Havre,
who's that player you brought here years ago, the hitter?
So few of us are good at what we do, and what we do,
well done or not, seems futile. I'm trying to find Monty
Holden's barber shop. I want to tell him style in anything,
pitching, hitting, cutting hair, is worth our trying even
if we fail. And when that style, the graceful compact swing
leaves the home crowd hearing its blood and the ball roars off
in night like determined moon, it is our pleasure
to care about something well done. If he doesn't understand
more than the final score, if he says, "After all, we won,"
I'll know my hair will not look right after he's done,
what little hair I have, what little time. And I'll drive home
knowing his windup was all show, glad I was there years back,
that I was lucky enough to be there when with one swing
you said to all of us, this is how it's done. The ball jumps
from your bat over and over. I want my poems to jump
like that. All poems. I want to say once to a world that feels
with reason it has little chance, well done. That's the lie
I cannot shout loud as this local truth: Well done, Mike. Dick.

Missoula Softball Tournament

RICHARD HUGO

This summer, most friends out of town
and no wind playing flash and dazzle
in the cottonwoods, music of the Clark Fork stale,
I've gone back to the old ways of defeat,
the softball field, familiar dust and thud,
pitcher winging drops and rises, and wives,
the beautiful wives in the stands, basic, used,
screeching runners home, infants unattended
in the dirt. A long triple sails into right center.
Two men on. Shouts from dugout: go, Ron, go.
Life is better run from. Distance to the fence,
both foul lines and dead center, is displayed.

I try to steal the tricky manager's signs.
Is hit-and-run the pulling of the ear?
The ump gives pitchers too much low inside.
Injustice? Fraud? Ancient problems focus
in the heat. Bad hop on routine grounder.
Close play missed by the team you want to win.
Players from the first game, high on beer,
ride players in the field. Their laughter
falls short of the wall. Under lights, the moths
are momentary stars, and wives, the beautiful wives
in the stands now take the interest they once feigned,
oh, long ago, their marriage just begun, years
of helping husbands feel important just begun,
the scrimping, the anger brought home evenings
from degrading jobs. This poem goes out to them.
Is steal-of-home the touching of the heart?
Last pitch. A soft fly. A can of corn
the players say. Routine, like mornings,

like the week. They shake hands on the mound.
Nice grab on that shot to left. Good game. Good game.
Dust rotates in their headlight beams.
The wives, the beautiful wives are with their men.

The Boxing Match

DAVID IGNATOW

Am I really a sports fan, I ask myself,
listening to the Dempsey-Firpo fight
over the radio and looking
at the open mouths of my friends:
Dempsey has just knocked Firpo out
of the ring, I am somewhat apathetic;
I can observe myself being surprised
but all the others are yelling with delight.
Of course I'm a sports fan, I assure myself.
Dempsey knocking Firpo out of the ring
is something I couldn't do. I could admit
that and admire strength. I fear it also
and I look around again and think
how if I scoffed at this hullabaloo
about a man being knocked out of the ring
these boys would turn on me and knock me down,
and I join in the yelling. Firpo
is climbing back into the ring
and I am glad for him
and admire him.

Ground Swell

MARK JARMAN

Is nothing real but when I was fifteen
going on sixteen, like a corny song?
I see myself so clearly then, and painfully —
knees bleeding through my usher's uniform
behind the candy counter in the theater
after a morning's surfing; paddling frantically
to top the brisk outsiders coming to wreck me,
trundle me gawkily along the beach floor's
gravel and sand; my knees ached with salt.
Is that all that I have to write about?
You write about the life that's vividest,
and if that is your own, that is your subject,
and if the years before and after sixteen
are colorless as salt and taste like sand —
return to those remembered chilly mornings,
the light spreading like a great skin on the water,
and the blue water scalloped with wind-ridges
and — what was it exactly? — that slow waiting
when, to invigorate yourself you peed
inside your bathing suit and felt the warmth
crawl all around your hips and thighs,
and the first set rolled in and the water level
rose in expectancy, and the sun struck
the water surface like a brassy palm,
flat and gonglike, and the wave face formed.
Yes. But that was a summer so removed
in time, so specially peculiar to my life,
why would I want to write about it again?
There was a day or two when, paddling out,
an older boy who had just graduated
and grown a great blond moustache, like a walrus,
skimmed past me like a smooth machine on the water,

and said my name. I was so much younger,
to be identified by one like him —
the easy deference of a kind of god
who also went to church where I did — made me
reconsider my worth. I had been noticed.
He soon was a small figure crossing waves,
the shawling crest surrounding him with spray,
whiter than gull feathers. He had said my name
without scorn, but just a bit surprised
to notice me among those trying the big waves
of the morning break. His name is carved now
on the black wall in Washington, the frozen wave
that grievers cross to find a name or names.
I knew him as I say I knew him, then,
which wasn't very well. My father preached
his funeral. He came home in a bag
that may have mixed in pieces of his squad.
Yes, I can write about a lot of things
besides the summer that I turned sixteen.
But that's my ground swell. I must start
where things began to happen and I knew it.

Say Goodbye to Big Daddy

RANDALL JARRELL

Big Daddy Lipscomb, who used to help them up
After he'd pulled them down, so that "the children
Won't think Big Daddy's mean"; Big Daddy Lipscomb,
Who stood unmoved among the blockers, like the Rock
Of Gibraltar in a life insurance ad,
Until the ball carrier came, and Daddy got him;
Big Daddy Lipscomb, being carried down an aisle
Of women by Night Train Lane, John Henry Johnson,
And Lenny Moore; Big Daddy, his three ex-wives,
His fiancée, and the grandfather who raised him
Going to his grave in five big Cadillacs;
Big Daddy, who found football easy enough, life hard enough
To — after his last night cruising Baltimore
In his yellow Cadillac — to die of heroin;
Big Daddy, who was scared, he said: "I've been scared
Most of my life. You wouldn't think so to look at me.
It gets so bad I cry myself to sleep —" his size
Embarrassed him, so that he was helped by smaller men
And hurt by smaller men; Big Daddy Lipscomb
Has helped to his feet the last ball carrier, Death.

The big black man in the television set
Whom the viewers stared at — sometimes, almost were —
Is a blur now; when we get up to adjust the set,
It's not the set, but a NETWORK DIFFICULTY.
The world won't be the same without Big Daddy.
Or else it will be.

139

Basketball

LOUIS JENKINS

A huge summer afternoon with no sign of rain. . . . Elm trees in the farmyard bend and creak in the wind. The leaves are dry and gray. In the driveway a boy shoots a basketball at a goal above the garage door. Wind makes shooting difficult and time after time he chases the loose ball. He shoots, rebounds, turns, shoots . . . on into the afternoon. In the silence between the gusts of wind the only sounds are the thump of the ball on the ground and the rattle of the bare steel rim of the goal. The gate bangs in the wind, the dog in the yard yawns, stretches and goes back to sleep. A film of dust covers the water in the trough. Great clouds of dust rise from open fields that stretch a thousand miles beyond the horizon.

Football

LOUIS JENKINS

I take the snap from center, fake to the right, fade back . . .
I've got protection. I've got a receiver open downfield. . . .
What the hell is this? This isn't a football, it's a shoe, a man's
brown leather oxford. A cousin to a football maybe, the same
skin, but not the same, a thing made for the earth, not the air.
I realize that this is a world where anything is possible and I
understand, also, that one often has to make do with what one
has. I have eaten pancakes, for instance, with that clear corn
syrup on them because there was no maple syrup and they
weren't very good. Well, anyway, this is different. (My man
downfield is waving his arms.) One has certain responsibili-
ties, one has to make choices. This isn't right and I'm not go-
ing to throw it.

Angling, a Day

GALWAY KINNELL

Though day is just breaking
when we fling two nightcrawlers
bunched on a hook as far out
as we can into Crystal Lake so leaden
no living thing could possibly swim through it
and let them lie on the bottom, under the water
and mist in which the doubled sun
soon shines and before long the doubled
mountains; though we drag Lake Parker
with fishing apparatus of several sorts,
catching a few yellow perch which we keep
just to have caught *something*; though
we comb with fine, and also coarse,
toothed hooks Shirley's Pond stocked
with trout famous for swallowing
any sharpened wire no matter
how expertly disguised as worm;
though we fish the fish-prowled pools
Bill Allen has divined by dip of bamboo
during all those misspent days trout-witching
Miller Run; and then cast some hours
away at the Lamoille, at the bend
behind Eastern Magnesia Talc Company's
Mill No. 4, which Hayden Carruth
says his friend John Engels says
is the best fishing around ("hernia bend,"
Engels calls it, on account of the weight
of fish you haul out of there); and end up
fishing the Salmon Hole of the Winooski
in which twenty-inch walleyes moil –
we and a dozen others who keep faith
with earth by that little string

which ties each person to the river at twilight —
casting and, as we reel in, twitching the rod,
our bodies curvetting in that curious motion
by which people giving fish motions to lures
look themselves like fish, until Fergus' jig,
catching a rock as he reels in,
houdinies out of its knot, and the man
fishing next to us, Ralph, reeling
somewhat himself due to an afternoon
of no fish and much Molson's ale,
lends us one of his, and with shaking hands
ties a stout knot between line and jig,
while a fellow from downcountry
goes on about how to free a snagged line
by sliding a spark plug down it —
"Well," Ralph says a couple of times,
"I sure never heard of that one,"
though sure enough, a few minutes later,
when Ralph's own line gets snagged,
he takes the fellow up on the idea,
borrows the man's spark plug, taps
the gap closed over the line as directed,
and lets her slide, yanking and flapping
vigorously as the spark plug disappears
into the water, and instantly loses spark plug
and jig both, and says, "Nope,
I sure never heard of that one" —
though, in brief, we have crossed the entire state
up at its thick end, and fished with hope
all the above-mentioned fishing spots
from before first light to after nightfall
and now will just be able to make it
to Essex Junction in time
to wait the several hours that must pass
before the train arrives in reality,
we have caught nothing — not counting,

of course, the three yellow perch Fergus
gave away earlier to Bill and Anne
Allen's cat Monsoon, who is mostly dead
along her left side though OK on her right,
the side she was probably lying on the night
last winter when, literally, she half froze to death –
and being afraid that Fergus, who's so tired
he now gets to his feet only to cast
and at once sits down, might be thoroughly
defeated, and his noble passion for fishing
broken, I ask him how he feels:
"I'm disappointed," he says, "but not discouraged.
I'm not saying I'm a fisherman, but fishermen know
there are days when you don't catch anything."

On the Tennis Court at Night

GALWAY KINNELL

We step out on the green rectangle
in moonlight; the lines glow,
which for many have been the only lines
of justice. We remember
the thousand trajectories the air has erased
of that close-contested last set —
blur of volleys, soft arcs of drop shots,
huge ingrown loops of lobs with topspin
which went running away, crosscourts recrossing
down to each sweet (and in exact proportion, bitter)
✪ in Talbert and Olds' *The Game of Doubles in Tennis.*
The breeze has carried them off but we still hear
the mutters, the doublefaulter's groans,
cries of "Deuce!" or "Love two!",
squeak of tennis shoes, grunt of overreaching,
all dozen extant tennis quips — "Just out!"
or, "About right for you?" or, "Want to change partners?"
and *baaah* of sheep translated very occasionally
into *thonk* of well-hit ball, among the pure
right angles and unhesitating lines
of this arena where every man grows old
pursuing that repertoire of perfect shots,
darkness already in his strokes,
even in death cramps waving an arm back and forth
to the disgust of the night nurse,
and smiling; and a few hours later found dead —
the smile still in place but the ice bag
she left on the brow now inexplicably
Scotchtaped to the right elbow — causing
all those bright trophies to slip permanently,
though not in fact much farther, out of reach,
all except the thick-bottomed young man

about to doublefault in soft metal on the windowsill:
"Runner-Up Men's Class B Consolation Doubles
St. Johnsbury Kiwanis Tennis Tournament 1969" . . .

Clouds come over the moon;
all the lines go out. November last year
in Lyndonville: it is getting dark,
snow starts falling, Zander Rubin wobble-twists
his worst serve out of the black woods behind him,
Stan Albro lobs into a gust of snow,
Dom Bredes smashes at where the ball theoretically
could be coming down, the snow blows down
and swirls about our legs, darkness flows
across a disappearing patch of green-painted asphalt
in the north country, where four men,
half-volleying, poaching, missing, grunting,
begging mercy of their bones, hold their ground,
as winter comes on, all the winters to come.

Horseback

CAROLYN KIZER

for Raymond Carver

Never afraid of those huge creatures
I sat sky-high on my western saddle
As we roared through the woods of skinny pine,
The clump clump of his great delicate hooves
Stirring up plumes of pine-needle dust,
One hand casual on the pommel,
The other plunged in the red coarse hair of his mane.

I recall the day he stopped dead on the trail
Trembling all over. We heard the chattering song
Of the rattler. My hypnotized bay
Couldn't move. Time stopped: The burnt odor of sage,
The smoky noon air, and the old old snake
As big around as my skinny wrist
Rising up from his rock.

Then the screen goes blank, and next it's summer camp:
I've conquered a wild mare, bare-back, whipping one arm
In sky-ward circles like a movie cowboy,
Screaming with joy.
So now when a stubborn skittery horse runs away with me
I give him his head. But as he tried to skin me off,
Plunging under low branches, I grit, "Oh no you don't!"

I bury my face in his neck, hang on for dear life,
Furious, happy, as he turns to race for home.
We pound into the stable yard and I dismount,
But wonder at curious glances turned my way
Until I see myself in the tack-room mirror,
My face a solid mass of purple welts.
Then I begin to sneeze and sneeze. My allergies

Burst into bloom, and I am forced to quit.
I don't sit a mount again for twenty years
Until I get to Pakistan
And Brigadier Effendi puts me up
On his perfect Arab mare.
My thighs tighten the old way as I marry a horse again . . .
I just wanted to tell you about it, Ray.

Winter Ball

AUGUST KLEINZAHLER

The squat man under the hoop
throws in short hooks, left-handed, right
in the dwindling sunlight as six lesbians
clown and shoot at the other end,
through a very loose game of three on three.

How pleased to be among themselves,
warm New Year's Day afternoon, neither young
nor graceful nor really good shots
but happy for the moment while a mutt
belonging to one of them runs

nearly out of its skin so glad to be
near the action and smells, vigorous and dumb
but keeping his orbits well-clear of the man
who would be a machine now if he could,
angling them in off both sides of the backboard.

You can tell this is a thing he's often done,
the boy who'd shoot till dusk
when starlings exploded, filthy birds,
from roost to roost, gathering only to fly off
at the first sharp sound, hundreds as one.

He'd wonder where they went at night
as he played his solitary game of *Round the World*,
sinking shots from along the perimeter,
then the lay-up, then the foul.
                    So intent at it
and grave it almost seemed like more than a game
with dark coming on and the cold.

Slam, Dunk, & Hook

YUSEF KOMUNYAKAA

Fast breaks. Lay ups. With Mercury's
Insignia on our sneakers,
We outmaneuvered the footwork
Of bad angels. Nothing but a hot
Swish of strings like silk
Ten feet out. In the roundhouse
Labyrinth our bodies
Created, we could almost
Last forever, poised in midair
Like storybook sea monsters.
A high note hung there
A long second. Off
The rim. We'd corkscrew
Up & dunk balls that exploded
The skullcap of hope & good
Intention. Bug-eyed, lanky,
All hands & feet . . . sprung rhythm.
We were metaphysical when girls
Cheered on the sidelines.
Tangled up in a falling,
Muscles were a bright motor
Double-flashing to the metal hoop
Nailed to our oak.
When Sonny Boy's mama died
He played nonstop all day, so hard
Our backboard splintered.
Glistening with sweat, we jibed
& rolled the ball off our
Fingertips. Trouble
Was there slapping a blackjack
Against an open palm.
Dribble, drive to the inside, feint,

& glide like a sparrow hawk.
Layups. Fast breaks.
We had moves we didn't know
We had. Our bodies spun

On swivels of bone & faith,
Through a lyric slipknot
Of joy, & we knew we were
Beautiful & dangerous.

Free Throw

MARK KRAUSHAAR

It's thirty years ago.
The sky's a sidewalk gray
and there's snow piled over the curbs.
The rule is the first to miss
hits ten more and the other goes inside
to keep count through the storm door.
Today it's you inside.
Your friend's mother sits drinking
colas and something. She's messy
and thin and when she looks up
you watch your friend's
breath make white trumpets at
the rim. He warms his hands
and shoots. A neighbor kid slips
and takes a dive on the ice.
Your friend hits three and misses
and shoots and misses and with each
shot the backboard jangles where the bolts
are loose. The mail arrives.
Your friend spins and shoots again
and misses and shoots
and when you think of it,
when you're quiet and think
of the whole scene now,
you think of the mailman's blue-
striped suit and trimmed mustache.
You think of his right arm resting
on a belt of keys. Of course,
here he's waiting with you,
beside you, for something — maybe
ten elegant, effortless hooks from your friend
or even your own miraculous set shot

straight over a mile-long cloud and a passing plane
then straight down and bouncing
off two chimneys and a telephone pole,
through that cheesy Sears hoop and
into your own outstretched right hand as gently
as that. Maybe your friend's
mother's watching with you. Or maybe
the kid next door jumps up off the ice
or the sun comes out
or there's a bird some place.
You begin again.
There isn't a sound.

400-Meter Freestyle

MAXINE KUMIN

The gun full swing the swimmer catapults and
  cracks

                                      s

                                        i

                                      x

feet away onto that perfect glass he catches at
a
n
 d
throws behind him scoop after scoop cunningly
  moving

                                     t

                                      h

                                   e

water back to move him forward. Thrift is his
  wonderful
 s
e
 c
ret; he has schooled out all extravagance. No muscle

                                      r

                                     i

                                    p

ples without compensation wrist cock to heel snap to
h
i
 s

mobile mouth that siphons in the air that nurtures

                                          h

                                            i

                                      m

at half an inch above sea level so to speak.
T
h
  e
astonishing whites of the soles of his feet rise

                              a

                                n

                              d

salute us on the turns. He flips, converts, and is gone
a
l
  l
  in one. We watch him for signs. His arms are steady
    at

                                          t

                                            h

                                            e

catch, his cadent feet tick in the stretch, they know
t
h
  e
lesson well. Lungs know, too; he does not list for

                                      a

                                        i

                                      r

  he drives along on little sips carefully expended
  b
u
  t

that plum red heart pumps hard cries hurt how soon

                                                            i

                                                              t

                                                          s

near one more and makes its final surge

                                        TIME: 4:25:9

To Swim, to Believe

MAXINE KUMIN

Centre College, Danville, Kentucky

The beautiful excess of Jesus on the waters
is with me now in the Boles Natatorium.
This bud of me exults, giving witness:

these flippers that rose up to be arms.
These strings drawn to be fingers.
Legs plumped to make my useful fork.

Each time I tear this seam to enter,
all that I carry is taken from me,
shucked in the dive.

Lovers, children, even words go under.
Matters of dogma spin off in the freestyle
earning that mid-pool spurt, like faith.

Where have I come from? Where am I going?
What do I translate, gliding back and forth
erasing my own stitch marks in this lane?

Christ on the lake was not thinking
where the next heel-toe went.
God did him a dangerous favor
whereas Peter, the thinker, sank.

The secret is in the relenting,
the partnership. I let my body work

accepting the dangerous favor
from this king-size pool of waters.
Together I am supplicant. I am bride.

The Advantages of Being a World Class Athlete

ANTHONY LACAVARO

In the end when the doctors circle around
Like doctors, they can find nothing wrong,

A perfect body they murmur over
And over like a prehistoric discovery,

Nothing wrong, nothing wrong except it's dead.
There will be no reason for this tragedy

Which catapults your death into the world
Of public myth: were you too good

For us, did they take you, or were you not
Of this earth to begin with and just returned.

The results of the tests say nothing about it,
Though one of the doctors speaking

Out of turn, will say softly,
"One foot appears to be larger than the other."

Halftime

ADAM LEFEVRE

October night nesting on the stadium.
The marching band blasts through a medley of moon songs, 4/4 time.
Moon River. Paper Moon.
Out from the ranks this year's appointed maiden spins,
twirling her silver baton.
Clusters of man-made little moons on poles
define the field she dances on.

[handwritten annotation: Lunar imagery]

She's heavy-thighed, not natural to the splits
and pirouettes she halfway does,
stumbling sometimes on the choppy turf.
In this town grace is not divine. It's work.

Her bosom, squeezed in a sequined leotard, heaves for air.
Her brow gleams with little gems of sweat.
She knows what's going wrong, and cares,
but has to keep up with the music till the end,
deferring shame like an inheritance.
Bass drum calmly counts the debt.
The unregenerate horns stampede.
She holds a shaky arabesque, hurls herself spread-eagle
through a wobble cartwheel.
A smile, immense and frozen, never leaves her face.
Her will to cheer remains sublime
to the tittering of the glockenspiel.

They don't ask much in this factory town.
Pity rises from the smokestacks, acknowledged waste.
All they want from their majorette is the dogged verity of a moon.
She must show,
spread her arms and smile at each degradation.
Bow deeply to the dropped baton.

Stick to it.
Graduate.
Raise sensible children with sensible names
like Jason Jr. and Dawn.
Teach them earthly virtues: bitterness, gravity.
Daughter into mother, always smiling,
reminding them this
is how it is, this
is how it ought to be.

The Right Cross

PHILIP LEVINE

The sun rising over the mountains
found me awake, found an entire valley
of sleepers awake, dreaming of a few hours
more of sleep. Though the Great Central Valley
is home for the homeless, the fruit pickers
of creation, for runaway housewives
bored by their husbands, and bored husbands,
the rising sun does not dip back behind
the Sierras until we're ready. The Valley sun
just comes on. We rise, drop our faces
in cold water, and face the prospects
of a day like the last one from which we
have not recovered. All this month I've
gone in search of the right cross, the punch
which had I mastered it forty years ago
might have saved me from the worst. The heavy bag
still hangs from the rafters of the garage,
turning in no wind, where my youngest son
left it when he went off ten years ago
abandoning his childish pursuits to me.
After tea, dry toast, and some toe-touching,
I'm ready to work. I pull on the salty
bag gloves, bow my head, dip one shoulder

into the great sullen weight, and begin
with a series of quick jabs. I'm up
on my toes, moving clockwise, grunting
as the blows crumple, the air going out
and coming back in little hot benedictions.
I'm remembering Nate Coleman barking
all those years ago, "Straight from the shoulder,
Levine," as though describing his own nature.

The gentlest man I ever knew, perfect
with his fists, our master and mentor,
who fought only for the love of it,
living secretly by day in suit and tie,
vending copper cookware from the back seat
of his black Plymouth. The dust rises
from the sour bag, and I feel how fragile
my left wrist has become, how meek the bones
of my shoulders as the shocks come home,
the bag barely moving. "Let it go!"
Nate would call, urging the right hand out
against the big light heavies, Marvin
with his sudden feints and blunt Becker,
his face grim and closed behind cocked fists.
Later, the gym gone silent in the half-dark,
Nate would stand beside me, left hand
on my shoulder, and take my right wrist
loosely in his right hand, and push it out
toward an imagined foe, his right knee
pressed behind my right knee until my leg
came forward. I could feel his words
— "like this" — falling softly on my cheek
and smell the milky sweetness of his breath
— "you just let it go" — the dark lashes
of his mysterious green eyes unmoving.
The bag is going now, swinging easily
with the force of jabs and hooks. The garage
moans as though this dance at its center
threatened to bring it down. I throw a right,
another, and another before I take my rest
in the cleared space amid the detritus
of five lives: boxes of unanswered letters,
school papers, report cards, scattered parts
of lawn mowers and motorcycles gone to ground.
The sky is coming through the mismatched boards
of the roof, pure blue and distant, the day

rising from the oily cement of the floor
as again I circle the heavy bag throwing out
more punches until I can't. If my sons
were here they'd cheer me on, and I'd
keep going into the impossible heat
and before I quit I might throw, just once,
for the first time, the perfect right cross.
They say it's magic. When it lands
you feel the force of your whole body,
even the deeper organs, the dark fluids
that go untapped for decades, the tiny
pale microbes haunting the bone marrow,
the intricate patterns that devised
the bones of the feet, you feel them
finally coming together like so many
atoms of salt and water as they form
an ocean or a tear, for just an instant
before the hand comes back under the chin
in its ordinary defensive posture.
The boys, the grown men dreaming
of the squared circle into which the light
falls evenly as they move without effort
hour after hour, breathing easily, oiled
with their own sweat, fight for nothing
except the beauty of their own balance,
the precision of each punch.
I hated to fight. I saw each blow
in a sequence of events leading
finally to a winner and a loser.
Yet I fought as boys were told to do,
and won and lost as men must. That's over.
Six months from my sixtieth year, doused
in my own juices, I call it quits
for the day, having earned the rituals —
the long bath, the shave, the laundered clothes,
the afternoon muse as the little clots

of stiffness break up and travel down
the channels of the blood. After dinner
and before sleep, I walk behind the garage
among grape vines and swelling tomatoes
to where the morning glories close down
in the rising darkness and the cosmos
flare their brilliant whites a last time
before the moon comes out. From under
the orange trees the click and chuckle
of quail; the tiny chicks dart out
for a last look and scurry back again
before the earth goes gray. A dove moans,
another answers from a distant yard as though
they called each other home, called each of us
back to our beds for the day's last work.

At the House of Ghosts

ADRIAN LOUIS

I'm back after twenty years of baiting the trap of the past. This is where I jitterbugged through the sagebrush to be in shape for fall football. Can I still do it? I jog ten yards. The saltgrass tackles me. My legs of iron are gone and my liver aches. Gasping, I stop at an irrigation ditch shrinking in deference to a land-locked seagull above my head. Under the Mason Valley sun, crawdads in the trickle of the ditch fight and flail. Their dancing claws snip bits of sky and lay blankets of shadow on their starving young. A small pool under the bank holds several giant thrashing carp. In a few days their lives will evaporate. I never liked carp, never loved crawdads.

I walk back to the house of ghosts. Here is the airless past that suffocated my youth. The shingles have shied away to show a black tarpaper slip. The remaining window panes have bullet holes in them. No doubt high school kids have partied here. Someone has rammed a car through one wall. In the kitchen sink, a fire has been made from an ancient *National Geographic.* My mother used to subscribe! A page of Himalayan snow is half-burned, browned into another page of Turkish poppies, red as the flame that narrowly missed them. On the floor is a pile of bird bones, feathers spit aside by some marauding cat. Near the avis carcass is a yellowed snapshot. It would be too perfect to say it was an old photo of me. It's some clown I've never seen. He's wearing the letterman's sweater of my old high school and is leaning against a '58 Fairlane with a brown-skinned cheerleader on his arm. He looks as strong as he ever will be. The world awaits him as it once awaited me.

The Midnight Tennis Match

THOMAS LUX

Note. In midnight tennis each player gets three serves
rather than the usual two.

You are tired
of this maudlin country club
and you are tired of his insults.
You'd like to pummel his forehead
with a Schweppes bottle
in the sauna, but instead
you agree, this time,
to meet him at midnight
on the tennis court.

When you get there
you can't see him
but you know he is waiting
on the other side of the net.
You consider briefly
his reputation.

You have first serve
so you run toward the net
and dive over it.
You land hard on your face.
It's not a good serve: looking up
you can barely see his white shorts
gleam in the darkness.

You get up, go back
to your side of the net
and dive over again.
This time you slide
to within a few feet of him.

Now you can make out his ankles
the glint of the moon
and his white socks.

Your last serve is the best:
your chin stops one inch
from the tip of his sneakers.
Pinheads of blood
bloom across your chest.
You feel good crawling
back to your side again.

Now it is his turn
and as he runs toward the net
you know he's the fastest man
you've ever seen.

His dive is of course flawless.
He soars by you,
goes completely off the court
and onto the lawn,
demolishing a few lounge chairs.
To finish, he slides
brilliantly onto the veranda.

You go up and sit beside him
and somehow
you don't feel too humiliated:
he is still unconscious.
At least now you know why
he is undefeated. It's
his sensitive, yet brutal, contempt.
With a similar contempt
you pour a gallon of water on his face.
He still has two more serves —

Cheap Seats, the Cincinnati Gardens, Professional Basketball, 1959

WILLIAM MATTHEWS

The less we paid, the more we climbed. Tendrils
of smoke lazed just as high and hung there, blue,
particulate, the opposite of dew.
We saw the whole court from up there. Few girls
had come, few wives, numerous boys in molt
like me. Our heroes leapt and surged and looped
and two nights out of three, like us, they'd lose.
But "like us" is wrong: we had no result
three nights out of three: so we had heroes.
And "we" is wrong, for I knew none by name
among that hazy company unless
I brought her with me. This was loneliness
with noise, unlike the kind I had at home
with no clock running down, and mirrors.

Foul Shots: A Clinic

WILLIAM MATTHEWS

for Paul Levitt

Be perpendicular to the basket,
toes avid for the line.

Already this description
is perilously abstract: the ball
and basket are round, the nailhead
centered in the centerplank
of the foulcircle is round,
and though the rumpled body
isn't round, it isn't
perpendicular. You have to draw
"an imaginary line," as the breezy

coaches say, "through your shoulders."
Here's how to cheat: remember
your collarbone. Now the instructions
grow spiritual — deep breathing,
relax and concentrate both; aim
for the front of the rim but miss it
deliberately so the ball goes in.
Ignore this part of the clinic

and shoot 200 foul shots
every day. Teach yourself not to be
bored by any boring one of them.

You have to love to do this, and chances
are you don't; you'd love to be good
at it but not by a love that drives
you to shoot 200 foul shots
every day, and the lovingly unlaunched

foul shots we're talking about now —
the clinic having served to bring us
together — circle eccentrically
in a sky of stolid orbits
as unlike as you and I are
from the arcs those foul shots
leave behind when they go in.

In Memory of the Utah Stars

WILLIAM MATTHEWS

Each of them must have terrified
his parents by being so big, obsessive
and exact so young, already gone
and leaving, like a big tipper,
that huge changeling's body in his place.
The prince of bone spurs and bad knees.

The year I first saw them play
Malone was a high school freshman,
already too big for any bed,
14, a natural resource.
You have to learn not to
apologize, a form of vanity.
You flare up in the lane, exotic
anywhere else. You roll the ball
off fingers twice as long as your
girlfriend's. Great touch for a big man,
says some jerk. Now they're defunct
and Moses Malone, boy wonder at 19,
rises at 20 from the St. Louis bench,
his pet of a body grown sullen
as fast as it grew up.

Something in you remembers every
time the ball left your fingertips
wrong and nothing the ball
can do in the air will change that.
You watch it set, stupid moon,
the way you watch yourself
in a recurring dream.

You never lose your touch
or forget how taxed bodies
go at the same pace they owe,
how brutally well the universe
works to be beautiful,
how we metabolize loss
as fast as we have to.

Good "D"

JAMES McKEAN

after Edward Hirsch

Their center blocks out and the ball
falls into his lap like the coach's book

says it will. Pivot, two-handed chest pass
to the outlet man, his flip

to a guard sprinting up the middle and the crowd
senses a break rolling at half court

and rises now for the finish, the jam
over a nondescript visitor

in knee wraps, invited to play in this gym
well lit on a Friday night in a state

that welcomes him and would send him packing
and bruised except he's hustled back

and turns in their key to wait — all taped fingers
and high tops — before the whole floor,

the forwards in their lanes pumping toward him
fast, two points on the stat sheets

written all over their faces, the guard dribbling
too high, head down as if he

needs a script, the guard who loves his right hand,
who pulls up late, who looks where he

passes, drunk on the home court's
din of expectation, everyone on their feet

for a goal good as given
over the nobody in his dull uniform

who stutter rushes the guard left, left
hand up, right down,

and releases the moment the pass is flung in panic,
the forward rising toward the basket

empty-handed because good defense reads well,
lives in the passing lane and lifts

the ball from beneath. Now, the forward,
who can't come down fast enough,

and the guard, suddenly tired, find far
up the floor the score turned,

the time gone and the crowd at a loss, fumbling
to sit back down, to say anything

for what's been stolen.

A Boy Juggling a Soccer Ball

CHRISTOPHER MERRILL

    after practice: right foot
to left foot, stepping forward and back,
    to right foot and left foot,
and left foot up to his thigh, holding
    it on his thigh as he twists
around in a circle, until it rolls
    down the inside of his leg,
like a tickle of sweat, not catching
    and tapping on the soft
side of his foot, and juggling
    once, twice, three times,
hopping on one foot like a jump-roper
    in the gym, now trapping
and holding the ball in midair,
    balancing it on the instep
of his weak left foot, stepping forward
    and forward and back, then
lifting it overhead until it hangs there;
    and squaring off his body,
he keeps the ball aloft with a nudge
    of his neck, heading it
from side to side, softer and softer,
    like a dying refrain,
until the ball, slowing, balances
    itself on his hairline,
the hot sun and sweat filling his eyes
    as he jiggles this way
and that, then flicking it up gently,
    hunching his shoulders
and tilting his head back, he traps it
    in the hollow of his neck,

and bending at the waist, sees his shadow,
    his dangling T-shirt, the bent
blades of brown grass in summer heat;
    and relaxing, the ball slipping
down his back . . . and missing his foot.

    He wheels around, he marches
over the ball, as if it were a rock
    he stumbled into, and pressing
his left foot against it, he pushes it
    against the inside of his right
until it pops into the air, is heeled
    over his head — the rainbow! —
and settles on his extended thigh before
    rolling over his knee and down
his shin, so he can juggle it again
    from his left foot to his right foot
— and right foot to left foot to thigh —
    as he wanders, on the last day
of summer, around the empty field.

The Diver

CHRISTOPHER MERRILL

was balanced on the edge of the platform
when a word appeared like a moon, gathered in clouds,
and swirled above his hands and eyes – he jumped
upwards and out, tucking his legs and head
into his body's shell and, somersaulting
backwards, searching the ceiling for a polestar,
he cracked his skull on the platform, nicking
the dormant seed of his own death, and dropped
feet first, head slumped, slicing through the air,
the water, bleeding from his mouth and ears,
to root himself on the bottom of the pool
and see the springboards fluttering in their sheaths,
the whole crowd on their feet, speaking in tongues,
a woman waving a broken fist or a flower,
then a light rising through the crimson water:
the sun the sailor takes his warning from.

Baseball and Writing

MARIANNE MOORE

Suggested by post-game broadcasts.

Fanaticism? No. Writing is exciting
and baseball is like writing.
   You can never tell with either
      how it will go
      or what you will do;
   generating excitement –
   a fever in the victim –
   pitcher, catcher, fielder, batter.
                Victim in what category?
*Owl*man watching from the press box?
              To whom does it apply?
              Who is excited? Might it be I?

It's a pitcher's battle all the way – a duel –
a catcher's, as, with cruel
   puma paw, Elston Howard lumbers lightly
      back to plate. (His spring
      de-winged a bat swing.)
   They have that killer instinct;
   yet Elston – whose catching
   arm has hurt them all with the bat –
            when questioned, says, unenviously,
"I'm very satisfied. We won."
            Shorn of the batting crown, says, "We";
            robbed by a technicality.

When three players on a side play three positions
and modify conditions,
   the massive run need not be everything.
      "Going, going . . ." Is
      it? Roger Maris

has it, running fast. You will
never see a finer catch. Well . . .
"Mickey, leaping like the devil" — why
            gild it, although deer sounds better —
snares what was speeding towards its treetop nest,
            one-handing the souvenir-to-be
            meant to be caught by you or me.

Assign Yogi Berra to Cape Canaveral;
he could handle any missile.
      He is no feather. "Strike . . . Strike *two!*"
            Fouled back. A blur.
            It's gone. You would infer
      that the bat had eyes.
      He put the wood to that one.
Praised, Skowron says, "Thanks, Mel.
      I think I helped a little bit."
                  All business, each, and modesty.
            Blanchard, Richardson, Kubek, Boyer.
                  In that galaxy of nine, say which
                  won the pennant? *Each.* It was he.

Those two magnificent saves from the knee — throws
by Boyer, finesses in twos —
      like Whitey's three kinds of pitch and pre-
            diagnosis
      with pick-off psychosis.
      Pitching is a large subject.
      Your arm, too true at first, can learn to
      catch the corners — even trouble
                  Mickey Mantle. ("Grazed a Yankee!
My baby pitcher, Montejo!"
                  With some pedagogy,
                  you'll be tough, premature prodigy.)

They crowd him and curve him and aim for the knees. Trying
indeed! The secret implying:
    "I can stand here, bat held steady."
        One may suit him;
        none has hit him.
    Imponderables smite him
    Muscle kinks, infections, spike wounds
    require food, rest, respite from ruffians. (Drat it!
            Celebrity costs privacy!)
Cow's milk, "tiger's milk," soy milk, carrot juice,
            brewer's yeast (high-potency) —
            concentrates presage victory

sped by Luis Arroyo, Hector Lopez —
deadly in a pinch. And "Yes,
    it's work; I want you to bear down,
        but enjoy it
        while you're doing it."
    Mr. Houk and Mr. Sain,
    if you have a rummage sale,
    don't sell Roland Sheldon or Tom Tresh.
            Studded with stars in belt and crown,
the Stadium is an adastrium.
            O flashing Orion,
            your stars are muscled like the lion.

When for Weeks the Sea Is Flat

RICK NOGUCHI

Wherever Kenji Takezo goes
He must surf
The perfect ride
In things that aren't waves.
This, the way he sees, is how
He survives, barely,
The world in which his balance is in
Constant peril. Last June
Kenji stood shirtless
After pedaling twice and gaining
Enough momentum on a blue Schwinn Cruiser.
He rode the 36th Street Hill
Goofyfoot: right toes forward
Curling the handle bars,
Left ball planted on the seat.
He cut curb to curb,
Dodging parked cars,
Leaning and controlling each turn
Until he gathered too much velocity.
Kenji developed
Speed wobbles.
He lost briefly
His style but continued to surf
The entire block,
The first person to go
Its length.
He then dumped the bike on the flats
Sliding after slamming
His belly against the asphalt.
He struggled to save the breath
That was knocked out of his lungs,
Even though the largest wave ever
Was not coming to drown him.

We Still Have Basketball, Sara

LISA OLSTEIN

That one long year we moved
in and out of each other's rooms
on the pick and roll, preferring a running game
to the slow down of half-court. If I said
your tendency was to choke in the clutch,
you might say mine was to look for fresh legs
down the stretch. Coming up against
the trading deadline and playoff divisions,
we broke down over technical fouls,
illegal defense violations. Now, whenever
the Knicks have a big game, I know where you are
and if they're playing the Celtics, you know
where I am too, and Sara, when I heard
about Ewing's broken wrist, I was sorry
I ever gloated over his bad knees.

Storm Surf

GREG PAPE

Rumor had it there had been
a hell of a storm or a tsunami
somewhere out in the Pacific,
one of those big, restless spirits
that visit the earth and carry off
whole populations and make a sudden mess
of everything in their path.
I stood on the beach with a borrowed board,
watching the great waves that dwarfed the pier
rise like glassy cliffs out of the fog.
I counted four or five surfers out there,
and now and then I saw one paddling hard
up a wave-face or streaking across a wall
in a crouch and disappearing in a tunnel
turning back into a wall. He was out there
somewhere, my mentor, the one I wanted
to be. We were to meet just offshore
of the continent, outside the farthest breaker,
there on the deep and restless, the saltwater
of origins and fates where we would ride
the elemental power of the turning earth,
our eyes, ears, mouths, hearts, and arms
open to fathom the purpose of the air
this very morning at eight. I waited,
shivering in my baggies, for a lull in the waves.

I took ten deep breaths, then ten more,
slow as resolve, and hit the water running
and bellied the board through the shore-break
and paddled out over the hiss and blather
of the soup that sounded like a chorus of the drowned.
I worked through the inside break, pumping

and paddling over crests, doing Hawaiian rolls,
washing back shoreward, half-flipping up
for air, laying a tired cheek on the grains
of sand caught in the paraffin until
what was grace was revised, and so much
effort made up of slight mistakes
in the face of a greater force turned
to doubt in the lines of sight glinting
from the brain, in the strings that pulled
the muscles that fumbled the strokes.
Grace changed too much may still
resemble grace, but hints of damage
in the way it moves.

It's hard to tell now, but it must have taken
an hour to get out past the pier
where the big waves rose stone-faced
out of the fog, not quite ready to break.
I straddled the board, rising up faces
and falling in troughs and calling
to the others, who must have had their fill
of doubt and secret glory and somehow
made it in while I, foolish, made it out.
The waves kept coming and breaking
before me until, even in the fog,
I could see clearly now the one I wanted to be,
beached and breathing, savoring the simple,
holding the broken halves of moments
carried out of the sea in strong
but humble arms.

Baseball

LINDA PASTAN

When you tried to tell me
baseball was a metaphor

for life: the long, dusty travail
around the bases, for instance,

to try to go home again;
the Sacrifice for which you win

approval but not applause;
the way the light closes down

in the last days of the season —
I didn't believe you.

It's just a way of passing
the time, I said.

And you said: that's it.
Yes.

Morning Athletes

MARGE PIERCY

for Gloria Nardin Watts

Most mornings we go running side by side
two women in mid-lives jogging, awkward
in our baggy improvisations, two
bundles of rejects from the thrift shop.
Men in their zippy outfits run in packs
on the road where we park, meet
like lovers on the wood's edge and walk
sedately around the corner out of sight
to our own hardened clay road, High Toss.

Slowly we shuffle, serious, panting
but talking as we trot, our old honorable
wounds in knee and back and ankle paining
us, short, fleshy, dark haired, Italian
and Jew, with our full breasts carefully
confined. We are rich earthy cooks
both of us and the flesh we are working
off was put on with grave pleasure. We
appreciate each other's cooking, each
other's art, photographer and poet, jogging
in the chill and wet and green, in the blaze
of young sun, talking over our work,
our plans, our men, our ideas, watching
each other like a pot that might boil dry
for that sign of too harsh fatigue.

It is not the running I love, thump
thump with my leaden feet that only
infrequently are winged and prancing,
but the light that glints off the cattails
as the wind furrows them, the rum cherries

reddening leaf and fruit, the way the pines
blacken the sunlight on their bristles,
the hawk circling, stooping, floating
low over beige grasses,

                      and your company
as we trot, two friendly dogs leaving
tracks in the sand. The geese call
on the river wandering lost in sedges
and we talk and pant, pant and talk
in the morning early and busy together.

Karate

STANLEY PLUMLY

If I could chop wood.
if I could just cut through
this furniture.

the paraphernalia
of blocks
and stacks of boards,
wedged and
piled
head-high,

if I could break the back
of a single two-by-four,

if the Japanese instructor would only
lay his little building
of bricks
in front of me,

if I could only drive nails
deep into the hard rose of the wood.

Nothing but Bad News

JENNIFER RICHTER

as the man next door on his porch
too small for bleachers or an ump
rolls up his shirtsleeves
grips the stick with both hands
raises it over his head to stretch
and the lovers downstairs
fire *What* What *What*
one-word argument that's lost the question
too many answers is the problem
with the name the doctors gave yesterday
to what's been eating you,
curveball that pushes me
back from the plate
the man next door taking
one hard swing after another
the dusk thickening
with fog, sweat, grill smoke
too much goddamn cheering
too many out there
laughing themselves sick

The Curlers at Dusk

DAVID RODERICK

At first we look like nomads plodding
against wind, black-booted, fur-clad,
with forty pound stones chained
to our backs, but we have come to shoot
in the hack, to hurl stones
over a glistening ice bed at dusk.
As our quoits slide across ice, one by one,
and knock against others or spin alone,
we bellow songs of warmth and swig
from bladder-bags of cider and gin.
With brooms we whisk ice-dust
to guide each stone into the *house*:
that faint target we stained to the river
with the blood of a barren sow.
See us now, caught in the torchlit glow
as the final quoit curls from the hand
of a bowed silhouette in the distance,
that decisive stone gliding
across ice, our shadows yoked
in the low arc of the fading light.

The Pike

THEODORE ROETHKE

The river turns,
Leaving a place for the eye to rest,
A furred, a rocky pool,
A bottom of water.

The crabs tilt and eat, leisurely,
And the small fish lie, without shadow, motionless,
Or drift lazily in and out of the weeds.
The bottom-stones shimmer back their irregular striations,
And the half-sunken branch bends away from the gazer's eye.

A scene for the self to abjure! —
And I lean, almost into the water,
My eye always beyond the surface reflection;
I lean, and love these manifold shapes,
Until, out from a dark cove,
From beyond the end of a mossy log,
With one sinuous ripple, then a rush,
A thrashing-up of the whole pool,
The pike strikes.

Sunday Skaters

MARY JO SALTER

These days,
the sky composes promises
and rips them to pieces. White
as a sheet, this morning's cloud-
cover crumples now and again, then snaps
back white when a gust shakes it out. Out
for the usual stroll,

I stop
to look at March in its muddles:
in a snowbank (black
boulders of old ice new-
mottled with powder), puddles
that must be from yesterday's
slanting rain and hail,

which fell
as if from one combined
salt-and-pepper shaker. I wind
as the wind does, chased downhill,
past the soaked, concrete blocks
of apartments and the dented heaps
of corrugated-iron houses

left out
in the rain for years and years,
the olive-green of their raised
surfaces sprayed with rust
in vertical bands. Venetian blinds —
more metal, pulled to metal sills, but
going against the grain —

                mix up
the texture, as does, still better, this
        one lace-curtained window fringed
                with icicles.
        Since they may melt in an hour,
on a day when everything's changed
        so often, one pauses for that pristine

                tension
of winter held in suspension. Just
        then, at the bottom of the street,
                I see the skaters:
        the luck of it
on a Sunday! The chances thin
        as the ice they coast on —

                to find
the snow wind-dusted off,
        and an hour both cold and warm enough
                overlapping leisure.
        From here, the disc of the pond
looks like one of those children's games
        designed for the palm,

                whose goal
is all at once to sink each silver
        ball into a hole.
                What each of them is slipping
        into, though, is another color:
approached, they glide by in mint and mauve
        and lilac, turquoise, rose, down

                parkas
in shiny nylon glimpsed
        for an instant. Like a clock
                with too many hands, gone haywire,

the pond's a rink of hockey sticks: tock-
tick-tick as the puck
    takes a shortcut from four to six

        to nine.
Look at that girl in the long braid, trailed
    by her mother, a close-cropped beauty
        who takes on a heart-speeding
    force, as they spin hand-in-
hand, and a teenager's sheen;
    and catch that baby buggy,

        pushed off
freely as a swing down the ice . . .
    Stock still at the clock's center,
        the pin that everything hinges on:
    the wide, fur-circled face
of a small boy who feels his place
    in the larger frame.

        It's all
about time, about time! Above us,
    a frosty layer of cloud takes the weight
        of the sun's one warming foot,
    bright as a yellow boot. Although,
as yet, nothing flies but the snow's
    negative (flurries

        of crows
appearing from nowhere), rather
    than wait for the other shoe
        to drop — that shower
    of rain, or sleet, or something, sure
to come — I rush into a coffee shop,
    and close the door.

        And close
my eyes, in time, when a cup
    of muddy, quivering liquid releases
        erasing clouds of steam, calling up
    in the sudden dark the skaters' dizzy
scissoring and see-sawing, scoring
        lines over, and over again.

Hits and Runs

CARL SANDBURG

I remember the Chillicothe ball players grappling the Rock
Island ball players in a sixteen-inning game ended by
darkness.

And the shoulders of the Chillicothe players were a red smoke
against the sundown and the shoulders of the Rock
Island players were a yellow smoke against the sun-
down.

And the umpire's voice was hoarse calling balls and strikes
and outs, and the umpire's throat fought in the
dust for a song.

Hook

FLOYD SKLOOT

My father limps on the leg that healed short.
His twice-broken right wrist, too weak to hold
a bowling ball palm up, is why he spins
a hook he cannot control. The ball rolls
slowly, as if limping while it wanders
from one gutter to the other and back.

We stand dead last in the Father and Son
League, not helped by my rocketing straight shots
that knock down nothing as often as they
knock down everything. He watches, giving
no advice. At thirteen, knowing there is
nothing for me to say either, I wait

for the ball's return so I can heft it
again and aim down the gleaming alley.

Blues for Benny Kid Paret

DAVE SMITH

For years I've watched the corners for signs.
A hook, a jab, a feint, the peekaboo prayer of forearms,
anything for the opening, the rematch I go on dreaming.
What moves can say your life is saved?

As I backpedaled in a field the wasps' nest waited,
playing another game: a child is peeping out of
my eyes now, confused by a rage of stinging,
wave after wave rising as I tell my fists to hurt me,
hurt the pain. I take my own beating, God help

me it hurts. Everything hurts, every punch darts,
jolts, enters my ears, bangs my temples. Who hurts
a man faster than himself? There was a wall I
bounced on, better than ropes. I was eleven years old.

In that year I saw the fog
turn aside and rise from the welts you were
to run away with its cousin the moon. They smacked
your chest and crossed your arms because you fell down
while the aisles filled with gorgeous women, high heels
pounding off like Emile, the Champion, who planted
his good two feet and stuck, stuck, stuck, stuck
until your brain tied up your tongue and your breath.

Somebody please, please I cried,
make them go away, but the ball in my hand was
feverish with the crackling light. I could not let go
as I broke against the wall. I was eleven years old.

Benny Paret, this night in a car ferrying
my load of darkness like a ring no one escapes,
I am bobbing and weaving in fog split only by a radio
whose harsh gargle is eleven years old, a voice in the air

telling the night you're down, counting time,
and I hear other voices, corners with bad moves
say *Get up you son of a bitch, get up and fight!* But you don't
get up again in my life and the only life you had is gone

with the moon I remember sailing down on your heart
where you lay in blood, waiting, photo flashes all snapped,
eyes open to take whatever is yet to come, jabs, hooks, cross
breaking through the best prayer you ever lifted to dump
you dizzied and dreamless in the green soft grass.

Softball at Julia Tutwiler Prison

R. T. SMITH

The pitcher shot her husband
and more than one felon
chatters zealously in the infield.
I come here once a month
with a busload of Episcopalians
to engage the women prisoners
on the dirt diamond of their yard.

They beat us every time,
depending on the hot arm
of a black girl from Wetumpka,
the dangerous base runners
and our reliable errors.
They have mastered this space.

Any shot knocked over the fence,
either fair or foul,
is a ground rules home run here.
Wardens always umpire,
fudging a bit for the visitors.
Irony is in the air.

In today's late innings
their shortstop has converted
to plug up our infield hole,
just to make things interesting.
They become generous
with the strange taste of winning.

In the makeshift dugout we share
talk runs from gothic novels
to Thanksgiving dinner.
Not a soul mentions escape
or athletic fellowship.

Now with two easy outs gone
in the ninth, I step up to bat,
eye the left field fence,
a smiling girl on the mound.
I have not hit safely all day,
but I want to change it all.

The ball is spinning slow motion.
I swing with every muscle
toward the fallen sun, swing
for guilt and the electric fence,
swing like hell for all of us.

Chin Music

ALAN SOLDOFSKY

The high hard one – up
and inside. The brush-back pitch
from which the batter reels out of the box.

Newcombe threw one, and Drysdale,
and Bob Gibson, who hurled smoke
in St. Louis. It was never an accident

like the other day in Detroit
when the A's rookie south paw
hit Kirk Gibson square in the mouth

with a fastball. He didn't go down,
but glared at the kid on the mound
then trotted to first, the blood

spilling from his mouth. It's a kind of honor,
a badge of toughness, to stand in
like that. Like the drivers who

pass you every now and then
on the two-lane, though they can't see
the collision coming toward them

up the hill that you can. The sky
a blue smear above the asphalt,
the fields of brown grass

being excavated into subdivisions
a few streets already paved
on which some of the kids will learn

bravado among cars, tempting fate,
standing in while everything
comes at them headlong.

Black Hair

GARY SOTO

At eight I was brilliant with my body.
In July, that ring of heat
We all jumped through, I sat in the bleachers
Of Romain Playground, in the lengthening
Shade that rose from our dirty feet.
The game before us was more than baseball.
It was a figure — Hector Moreno
Quick and hard with turned muscles,
His crouch the one I assumed before an altar
Of worn baseball cards, in my room.

I came here because I was Mexican, a stick
Of brown light in love with those
Who could do it — the triple and hard slide,
The gloves eating balls into double plays.
What could I do with fifty pounds, my shyness,
My black torch of hair, about to go out?
Father was dead, his face no longer
Hanging over the table or our sleep,
And mother was the terror of mouths
Twisting hurt by butter knives.

In the bleachers I was brilliant with my body,
Waving players in and stomping my feet,
Growing sweaty in the presence of white shirts.
I chewed sunflower seeds. I drank water
And bit my arm through the late innings.
When Hector lined balls into deep
Center, in my mind I rounded the bases
With him, my face flared, my hair lifting
Beautifully, because we were coming home
To the arms of brown people.

My Grandfather's Cap

DAVID ST. JOHN

There are so few photographs of him,
Peter Fries, my Mother's quiet
Father, baker and bar owner, patriarch
Of silence and five daughters, one son,
And a past distinguished, I discover,
Late one night rummaging haphazardly
Through an old bureau drawer,
A secret life in baseball. Along
The huge arm
Of the old horsehair sofa,
I lay three snapshots: two of Pete
Off fishing with some pals
High in the Sierras; and the last,
His team photo, taken some early
Summer evening, before the season's
Last minor league game . . .
He's stretched out, leaning on one elbow,
Surrounded by his boyish teammates,
Himself, even more boyish,
His jersey scripted with the sponsor's
Name, *Bittels*, and his soft felt cap —
The one I remember hooked
On the metal barb jutting off the coat rack
Just inside the door, the one
With the ghost of a "B" along its crown,
Signifying my entire childhood —
Pulled down over one eye,
Just like a displaced Bowery Boy.
In that first fishing shot, he's wearing
A straw hat and looking for all the world,
I'm afraid, quite frighteningly
Like Maurice Chevalier . . .
Sitting on a huge fallen log

Between two friends, squinting
Into the diamond of the camera lens
In the high mountain sunlight at the lake's
Edge. In the second, he's squatting
Indian style on the flat
Ancient wood of an anonymous pier,
His five jaunty buddies hamming it up
With rods and buckets, but not
A single caught fish anywhere in sight!
It's this one I keep holding up
To the glare of the crook-necked lamp,
Trying to make out in the faded sepia
Of this muddy print
The crumpled cap he's wearing,
Pulled down over the same narrow slit
Of an eye, half closed, half winking,
A cap suspiciously familiar
Even though it's twenty years later —
His old baseball cap, its felt worn
To an oily shine, a shine like those scales
Strewn along the planks at his feet,
Pale stars weighing
Almost nothing in the air and light,
Weighing less, even, than an early
Summer evening settling
Around a boy in a wool jersey with a life
As yet unreckoned, the crowd noise
Slowly rising as the crack of the bat
Lifts a tiny white balloon
Into the sky, as he runs, breathless, alone
Stretching as far as his body will allow
Into my present, our lines striking
The water of the sky, both of us reaching
For those stilled, carefully stitched
Seams of this yet distant, yet pale, future
And now forever-rising moon.

Run before Dawn

WILLIAM STAFFORD

Most mornings I get away, slip out
the door before light, set forth on the dim, gray
road, letting my feet find a cadence
that softly carries me on. Nobody
is up — all alone my journey begins.

Some days it's escape: the city is burning
behind me, cars have stalled in their tracks,
and everybody is fleeing like me but some other direction.
My stride is for life, a far place.

Other days it is hunting: maybe some game will cross
my path and my stride will follow for hours, matching
all turns. My breathing has caught the right beat
for endurance; familiar trancelike scenes glide by.

And sometimes it's a dream of motion, streetlights coming near,
passing, shadows that lean before me, lengthened
then fading, and a sound from a tree: a soul, or an owl.

These journeys are quiet. They mark my days with adventure
too precious for anyone else to share, little gems
of darkness, the world going by, and my breath, and the road.

Schsssssss

MARTÍN STEINGESSER

schusssssssss

swoop

– steel

edge/to/ice/edge –
d
o
w   up
n

hanging
over

the world
between outspread arms

below
trees like dark fur
on a small
bear
so
still
closeby gray barkblur
and the distance
still
and clear
clear as a
tink
of ice
across the blue
snow mountain
air

Swinging on the First Pitch

DABNEY STUART

You go up there cocked.
You don't care if the whole
stadium knows you're hitting away.
After all, he's been bringing
the first one in from the start.
There's no need to look
it over. It's the same stuff
you've been taking all day, all
season, since you can remember.
So what if the two of you keep
leading the league in strikeouts,
at least this time he's not getting
ahead of you while you stand there
taking up space. Anybody
can do that, that's what other people
buy tickets for.
If he doesn't groove it, you're sure
it'll be in the strike zone,
or near, and the way you feel
it could be a mile off and you'd still
go with it, dump it down the line
for a double. You're ready
for anything he's got, dug in, rippling
the air, wrists rolling smooth
in the box ready
for anything.
He goes into his motion —
the same old cunnythumb herkyjerk
sidesaddle nonsense, nothing
up his sleeve but what you've known
is there all along — winds,
delivers. It's a fast ball,

big as a globe, 110
miles an hour, coming
right at your head.

Lousy in Center Field

JAMES TATE

Thank God
the manager is blind,
the coach is deaf
and the owner dead:
I am free

to completely ignore
the ball, I invoke
my mental dropsy
to communicate to the crowd:
they no longer concern me.

Breaking into an easy stride,
I'm frozen once again
in an attitude of unfortunate
interior crumbling mouseholes.
The ball is hit, impersonal

into the gnawing, cobwebby air.
I'm feeling naughty and falter
like an enormous filing cabinet
in an ashen center field.
And, like an entangled puppet

wriggling at the hairdresser,
I chatter before abrupt sleep.

Shadowboxing

JAMES TATE

Sometimes you almost get a punch in.
Then you may go for days without even seeing him,
or his presence may become a comfort
for a while.

He says: I saw you scrambling last night
on your knees and hands.

He says: How come you always want to be
something else, how come you never take your life
seriously?

And you say: Shut up! Isn't it enough
I say I love you, I give you everything!

He moves across the room with his hand
on his chin, and says: How great you are!

Come here, let me touch you, you say.

He comes closer. Come closer, you say.
He comes closer. Then. *Whack!* And
you start again, moving around and around
the room, the room which grows larger
and larger, darker and darker. The black moon.

Forty-one Seconds on a Sunday in June, in Salt Lake City, Utah

QUINCY TROUPE

for Michael Jordan

rising up in time, michael jordan hangs like an icon, suspended in
    space,
cocks his right arm, fires a jump shot for two, the title game on the line,
his eyes two radar screens screwed like nails into the mask of his face

bore in on the basket, gaze focused, a thing of beauty, no shadow, or
    trace,
no hint of fear, in this, his showplace, his ultimate place to shine,
rising up in time michael jordan hangs like an icon, suspended in space,

after he has moved from baseline to baseline, sideline to sideline, his
    coal-face
shining, wagging his tongue, he dribbles through chaos, snaking
    serpentine,
his eyes two radar screens screwed like nails into the mask of his face,

he bolts a flash up the court, takes off, floats in for two more in this race
for glory, it is his time, what he was put on earth for, he can see the
    headline,
rising up in time, michael jordan hangs like an icon, suspended in
    space,

inside his imagination, he feels the moment he will embrace, knows his
    place
is written here, inside this quickening pace of nerves, he will define,
his eyes two radar screens screwed like nails into the mask of his face,

inside this moment he will rule on his own terms, quick as a cat he
    interfaces

time, victory & glory, as he crosses over his dribble he is king of this
   shrine,
rising up in time, michael jordan hangs like an icon, suspended in
   space,
his eyes two radar screens screwed like nails into the mask of his face

Poem for My Father; for Quincy Troupe, Sr.

QUINCY TROUPE

father, it was an honor to be there, in the dugout
with you, the glory of great black men swinging their lives
as bats at tiny white balls
burning in at unbelievable speeds, riding up & in & out
a curve falling off the table, moving away screwing its stitched
magic into chitlin circuit air, its comma seams spinning
towards break down, dipping, like a hipster
bebopping a knee-dip stride in the charlie parker forties
wrist curling behind a "slick" black back
like a swan's neck, cupping
an invisible ball of dreams —

father, & you there regal as an african obeah man sculpted
out of wood, from a tree of no name no place origin
thick roots branching down into cherokee & someplace else lost
way back in africa, the sap running dry
crossing from north carolina, into georgia, in grandmother mary's womb
your mother in the violence of that red soil, ink blotter
gone now into blood graves of american news sponging
rococo truth dead & long gone as dinosaurs
the agent-oranged landscape of former names
absent of polysyllables, dry husk consonants there
now, in their place, flat as polluted rivers
& that guitar string smile always snaking across virulent
american red neck faces scorching, like atomic
heat mushrooming over nagasaki & hiroshima
those fever blistered shadows of it all
inked into sizzling concrete

but you there father, a yardbird solo riffin on
bat & ball glory, breaking down the fabricated myths
of white major league legends, of who was better

than who, beating them at their own crap
game with killer bats, as bud powell swung his silence into beauty
of a josh gibson home run skittering across the piano keys
of bleachers, shattering all fabricated legends up there in lights
struck-out white knights running the risky edge of amazement
awe, the miraculous truth sluicing through
steeped in the blues, confluencing, like the point
at the cross between a fastball disguised as a curve
sliding away in a wicked sly grin, posed as an ass scratching
uncle tom, like satchel paige delivering his hesitation pitch,
then coming back with a hard high fast one
quicker than a professional hit-
man, the deadliness of it all, the strike
like that of the brown bomber's, or sugar
ray robinson's lightning, cobra bite

& you there father, catching rhythms of chano pozo
balls, drumming into your catcher's mitt
fast as "cool papa" bell jumping into bed
before the lights went out

of the old negro baseball league, a promise
a harbinger, of shock waves, soon to come

The Jump Shooter

DENNIS TRUDELL

The way the ball
hung there
against the blue or purple

one night last week
across town
at the playground where

I had gone to spare
my wife
from the mood I'd swallowed

and saw in the dusk
a stranger
shooting baskets a few

years older maybe
thirty-five
and overweight a little

beer belly saw him
shooting there
and joined him didn't

ask or anything simply
went over
picked off a rebound

and hooked it back up
while he
smiled I nodded and for

ten minutes or so we
took turns
taking shots and the thing

is neither of us said
a word
and this fellow who's

too heavy now and slow
to play
for any team still had

the old touch seldom
ever missed
kept moving further out

and finally his t-shirt
a gray
and fuzzy blur I stood

under the rim could
almost hear
a high school cheer

begin and fill a gym
while wooden
bleachers rocked he made

three in a row from
twenty feet
moved back two steps

faked out a patch
of darkness
arched another one and

the way the ball
hung there
against the blue or purple

then suddenly filled
the net
made me wave goodbye

breathe deeply and begin
to whistle
as I walked back home.

Pitching Coups

RON WELLBURN

The arc of the pitching arm
unwinds a circle of dreams
and corkscrews out behind a kick
to release a flying head,
in whose face coming towards
the men with bats
is a leer and a laugh.
The stitches of the sphere blur
into war paint and the head's
ecstatic yell echoes
throughout this canyon of battle.
It flies as straight as an arrow or
whirls like a tomahawk;
sometimes it just jumps off a ledge
the way lovers are said to do
in secret ravines all over the country.
It always comes ready to count coup
and tease and intimidate.
The pitching arm belongs to coyote
and so does the flying head.
The arm belongs to Chief Bender
from yesterday, then Allie Reynolds,
and the next time to Cal McLish,
and now to John Henry Johnson and
Fernando, the Valenzuela.
Pitchers all.
Coyotes too.
'Skins.

Running

RICHARD WILBUR

I. 1933
(North Caldwell, New Jersey)

What were we playing? Was it prisoner's base?
I ran with whacking keds
Down the cart-road past Rickard's place,
And where it dropped beside the tractor-sheds

Leapt out into the air above a blurred
Terrain, through jolted light,
Took two hard lopes, and at the third
Spanked off a hummock-side exactly right,

And made the turn, and with delighted strain
Sprinted across the flat
By the bull-pen, and up the lane.
Thinking of happiness, I think of that.

II. Patriots' Day
(Wellesley, Massachusetts)

Restless that noble day, appeased by soft
Drinks and tobacco, littering the grass
While the flag snapped and brightened far aloft,
We waited for the marathon to pass,

We fathers and our little sons, let out
Of school and office to be put to shame.
Now from the street-side someone raised a shout,
And into view the first small runners came.

Dark in the glare, they seemed to thresh in place
Like preening flies upon a window-sill,
Yet gained and grew, and at a cruel pace
Swept by us on their way to Heartbreak Hill —

Legs driving, fists at port, clenched faces, men,
And in amongst them, stamping on the sun.
Our champion Kelley, who would win again,
Rocked in his will, at rest within his run.

iii. Dodwells Road
(Cummington, Massachusetts)

I jog up out of the woods
To the crown of the road, and slow to a swagger there,
The wind harsh and cool to my throat,
A good ache in my rib-cage.

Loud burden of streams at run-off,
And the sun's rocket frazzled in blown tree-heads:
Still I am part of that great going,
Though I stroll now, and am watchful.

Where the road turns and debouches,
The land sinks westward into exhausted pasture.
From fields which yield to aspen now
And pine at last will shadow,

Boy-shouts reach me, and barking.
What is the thing which men will not surrender?
It is what they have never had, I think,
Or missed in its true season,

So that their thoughts turn in
At the same roadhouse nightly, the same cloister,
The wild mouth of the same brave river
Never now to be charted.

You, whoever your are,
If you want to walk with me you must step lively.
I run, too, when the mood offers,
Though the god of that has left me.

But why in the hell spoil it?
I make a clean gift of my young running
To the two boys who break into view,
Hurdling the rocks and racing,

Their dog dodging before them
This way and that, his yaps flushing a pheasant
Who lifts now from the blustery grass
Flying full tilt already.

At the Ball Game

WILLIAM CARLOS WILLIAMS

The crowd at the ball game
is moved uniformly

by a spirit of uselessness
which delights them —

all the exciting detail
of the chase

and the escape, the error
the flash of genius —

all to no end save beauty
the eternal —

So in detail they, the crowd,
are beautiful

for this
to be warned against

saluted and defied —
It is alive, venomous

it smiles grimly
its words cut —

The flashy female with her
mother, gets it —

The Jew gets it straight — it
is deadly, terrifying —

It is the Inquisition, the
Revolution

It is beauty itself
that lives

day by day in them
idly −

This is
the power of their faces

It is summer, it is the solstice
the crowd is

cheering, the crowd is laughing
in detail

permanently, seriously
without thought

Autumn Begins in Martins Ferry, Ohio

JAMES WRIGHT

In the Shreve High football stadium,
I think of Polacks nursing long beers in Tiltonsville,
And gray faces of Negroes in the blast furnace at Benwood,
And the ruptured night watchman of Wheeling Steel,
Dreaming of heroes.

All the proud fathers are ashamed to go home.
Their women cluck like starved pullets,
Dying for love.

Therefore,
Their sons grow suicidally beautiful
At the beginning of October,
And gallop terribly against each other's bodies.

Notes on Contributors

Diane Ackerman is the author of seventeen works of poetry and prose, including, most recently, *I Praise My Destroyer*.

Kim Addonizio's latest book of poems is *Tell Me*. She is coauthor, with Dorianne Laux, of *The Poet's Companion: A Guide to the Pleasures of Writing Poetry*. Her book of stories, *In the Box Called Pleasure*, was recently published by FC2.

Elizabeth Alexander is the author of *The Venus Hottentot* and *Body of Life* as well as many essays and articles on African American literature and culture.

Sherman Alexie's new collection of poetry and short stories was published in 2000 by Hanging Loose Press and Grove/Atlantic, respectively. He is working on a film adapted from his novel *Reservation Blues*.

Agha Shahid Ali is a professor of creative writing at the University of Utah. His latest book of poems is *The Country without a Post Office*. His anthology *Ravishing Disunities: Real Ghazals in English*, was published in 2000.

Sam Allen lives in the Boston area.

Craig Arnold's first book, *Shells*, won the 1999 Yale Younger Poets Award.

George Barlow is a graduate of the University of Iowa Writers' Workshop. He is the author of *Gabriel* and *Gumbo*, a National Poetry series selection, and is currently associate professor of American studies and English at Grinnell College.

Dorothy Barresi is the author of *All of the Above* and *The Post-Rapture Diner*, which won an American Book Award. Her poems and essays have appeared in the *Harvard Review*, *Parnassus*, the *Gettysburg Review*, *Volt*, and *Poetry*. She is chair of the Creative Writing Program at California State University, Northridge. She lives in Los Angeles with her husband and sons.

Marvin Bell has been a faculty member at the Iowa Writers' Workshop for thirty-five years. He now teaches half the year in Iowa City and apportions the rest of his time between the East and the Northwest. His many books include poetry, essays, and a correspondence in poetry with William Stafford. He ran the Honolulu Marathon in 1979.

Elizabeth Bishop's first book, *North & South*, won the Houghton Mifflin Poetry Award for 1946. In 1955 she received the Pulitzer Prize for *Poems: North & South—A Cold Spring*. Her next book of poetry, *Questions of Travel*, won the

National Book Award. *Geography III* received the National Book Critics Circle Award. In 1976 Bishop became both the first American and the first woman to win the Books Abroad/Neustadt Prize for Literature. She served as a consultant in poetry to the Library of Congress in 1949–50. Bishop died on October 6, 1979. Posthumous works include *The Complete Poems, 1927–1979* and *The Collected Prose*.

Kendra Borgmann recently graduated from the M.F.A. program at the University of Massachusetts, Amherst. Her poems have appeared in *Grand Street* and *Cutbank* and on *The Poetry Daily Web Site*. She currently lives in Amherst.

Kevin Bowen is the director of the William Joiner Center for the Study of War and its Social Consequences at University of Massachusetts-Boston. He is also the author, translator, and editor of several books of poetry.

Catherine Bowman's work has appeared in the *Paris Review*, the *Kenyon Review*, *TriQuarterly*, *River Styx*, and *The Best American Poetry, 1989, 1994, 1995*. Her collections include *1-800-HOT-RIBS*, which won the Perrigine Smith Poetry Prize and the Kate Frost Tufts Discovery Award, and *Rock Farm*. She currently lives and teaches in Bloomington, Indiana, and hosts a series on poetry for National Public Radio's *All Things Considered*.

Ralph Burns's last book, *Swamp Candles*, won the Iowa Poetry Award and was published by the University of Iowa Press in 1996. His most recent poems have appeared in *Field*, *Brilliant Corners*, and *Poetry International*. He edits *CRAZYHORSE*.

Douglas Carlson's essays have appeared recently in the *Georgia Review*, *Ascent*, and the *American Literary Review*. In spring 1999 the University of Utah Press published his coauthored *When We Say We're Home*. He teaches at Concordia College in Moorhead, Minnesota.

Hayden Carruth has won the National Book Award, the National Book Critics Circle Award, a 1995 Lannan Literary Award, the Shelley Memorial Award, and fellowships from the Guggenheim Foundation and the NEA, among many other honors. The author of dozens of books of poetry and prose, he is a former editor of *Poetry* and former poetry editor for *Harper's*. He lives in Munnsville, New York.

Raymond Carver's first collection of stories, *Will You Please Be Quiet, Please* (a National Book Award nominee in 1977), was followed by *What We Talk about When We Talk about Love, Cathedral* (nominated for the Pulitzer Prize in 1984), and *Where I'm Calling From* in 1988, when he was inducted into the American

Academy of Arts and Letters. He died in August of that year, shortly after completing the poems of *A New Path to the Waterfall.*

Olena Kalytiak Davis's poems have appeared in the *New England Review,* the *Northwest Review,* the *North American Review, Poetry Northwest,* and *Best American Poetry 1995.* She has also been nominated for several Pushcart Prizes. *And Her Soul out of Nothing,* her first book, was selected by Rita Dove for the 1997 Brittingham Prize in Poetry and was published by the University of Wisconsin Press. She currently resides in Juneau, Alaska.

Mike Delp's most recent book is *The Coast of Nowhere: Meditations on Rivers, Lakes and Streams,* published by Wayne State University Press.

James Dickey is the author of *Deliverance* as well as several other novels and fifteen books of poetry. His many honors include the National Book Award and a Melville Cane Award for *Buckdancer's Choice.* He was invited to read at President Carter's inauguration in 1977 and most recently served as judge of the prestigious Yale Younger Poets series. He died in 1997 in South Carolina.

Norman Dubie is the author of twenty books. He teaches at Arizona State University.

Stephen Dunn is the author of twelve collections of poetry, including *Different Hours.*

Cornelius Eady is the author *of You Don't Miss Your Water; The Gathering of My Name,* a Pulitzer Prize nominee; *BOOM BOOM BOOM; Victims of the Latest Dance Craze,* which was the Lamont Poetry selection of the Academy of American Poets; and *Kartunes.* His honors include the Prairie Schooner Strousse Award and fellowships from the Guggenheim Foundation, the National Endowment for the Arts, the Rockefeller Foundation, and the Lila Wallace–Reader's Digest Foundation. He lives in New York City and is the director of the poetry center at the State University of New York at Stony Brook.

John Engels teaches at St. Michael's College in Vermont. His latest collection is *Sinking Creek.*

Martín Espada's fifth book of poems, *Imagine the Angels of Bread,* won an American Book Award and was a finalist for the National Book Critics Circle Award. His most recent collection is *A Mayan Astronomer in Hell's Kitchen.* His poems have appeared in *Harper's,* the *Nation,* the *New York Times Book Review,* and *The Best American Poetry.* His first book of essays, *Zapata's Disciple,* received an Independent Publisher Book Award. A former tenant lawyer, Espada currently teaches in the English Department at the University of Massachusetts at Amherst.

David Allan Evans met James Dickey at a writers' conference in Boulder when he was in his late twenties. When he showed Dickey his pole vaulter poem at the conference, Dickey told him, "Shakespeare never did any pole vaulting."

B. H. Fairchild has received an NEA Fellowship in Poetry, a California Arts Grant, a Walter E. Dakin Fellowship to the Sewanee Writers' Conference, a National Writers Union First Prize, an AWP Anniversary Award, and the 1996 Capricorn and 1997 Beatrice Hawley Awards for *The Art of the Lathe*, which was a finalist for the 1998 National Book Award for Poetry and is the winner of the 1999 Kingsley Tufts Poetry Award. His other poetry collections include *Local Knowledge, The System of Which the Body Is One Part, Flight*, and *The Arrival of the Future*. He is also the author of *Such Holy Song*, a study of William Blake. He lives with his wife and daughter in Claremont, California.

Lawrence Ferlinghetti is the cofounder of City Lights Bookstore and its imprint, City Lights Books, which have thrived in San Francisco's North Beach neighborhood since 1953. He is the author of over twenty books of poetry, plays, prose, and translations.

Gary Fincke is the Writers Institute director at Susquehanna University. His most recent books are the *Almanac for Desire* and *Blood Ties*.

Robert Francis taught at summer workshops and conferences and universities across the United States. His works include *Stand with Me Here; Like Ghosts of Eagles: Poems 1966–1974;* a novel, *We Fly Away;* and an autobiography, *The Trouble with Francis*. He won the Shelley Memorial Award in 1939 and died in 1987.

Carol Frost is the author of several books of poems, most recently *Love & Scorn*. She has received several fellowships from the National Endowment for the Arts, and her writing has been honored by several organizations. Her essays and poems regularly appear in the *Atlantic Monthly*, the *American Poetry Review*, the *Gettysburg Review, Shenandoah*, the *Southern Review*, the *Kenyon Review*, the *New England Review*, and the *New York Times*. She currently directs the Catskill Poetry Workshop at Hartwick College, where she is writer-in-residence, and lives in upstate New York with her husband, the poet Richard Frost. They have two sons.

Brendan Galvin's recent books are *The Strength of the Named Thing* and *Sky and Island Light*, both from Louisiana State University Press, and the narrative poem *Hotel Malabar*, winner of the 1997 Iowa Prize. He lives in Truro, Massachusetts.

James Galvin's most recent collection of poems is *Resurrection Update*. He has been awarded numerous fellowships and is the author of the critically acclaimed prose book *The Meadow*. He lives in Tie Siding, Wyoming, and in Iowa City, where he teaches at the University of Iowa Writers' Workshop.

Gary Gildner lives and writes on a ranch in Idaho's Clearwater Mountains. His seventeen published books include *Blue Like the Heavens: New & Selected Poems*, *The Second Bridge* (a novel), *A Week in South Dakota* (short stories), *The Warsaw Sparks* (a memoir about coaching a baseball team in Communist Poland), and *The Bunker in the Parsley Fields*, which received the 1996 Iowa Poetry Prize. He has also received the National Magazine Award for Fiction, a Pushcart Prize, the Robert Frost Fellowship, and the William Carlos Williams and Theodore Roethke poetry prizes. At the age of sixteen he threw an American Legion no-hitter. For more information, see *World Authors 1985–1990*.

Louise Glück's poetry has received the Pulitzer Prize, the Poetry Society of America's William Carlos Williams Award, the Rebekah Johnson Bobbitt National Prize for poetry, the National Book Critics Circle Award, the Boston Globe Literary Press Award, and the Poetry Society of America's Melville Kane Award. She has also published a collection of essays, *Proofs and Theories: Essays on Poetry*, which won the PEN/Martha Albrand Award for Nonfiction. In 1999 she was elected a chancellor of the Academy of American Poets.

Linda Gregerson, a former actress and editor, teaches American poetry and Renaissance literature at the University of Michigan in Ann Arbor.

Thom Gunn was born in 1929 in Britain and raised in wartime London. He has been a senior lecturer in English at the University of California at Berkeley for many years and has lived in San Francisco since 1961. His most recent book, *The Man with Night Sweats*, centers on street people and people with AIDS. Thom Gunn is a recipient of a MacArthur Fellowship.

Donald Hall's most recent book of poetry is *The Old Life*. He is the author of twelve other volumes of poetry and many books of prose. He continues to inhabit the old farmhouse, occupied by his family for generations, where he and Jane Kenyon lived.

Forrest Hamer is the author of *Call & Response*, which won the Beatrice Hawley Award, *Terrain* with Dan Bellam and Molly Fisk, and *Middle Ear*.

Michael S. Harper's most recent book is *Songlines in Michaeltree: New and Collected Poems*. He is coeditor of *The Vintage Book of African American Poetry* and university professor and professor of English at Brown University, where he has taught since 1970. From 1988 to 1993 he served as Rhode Island's first poet laureate.

Jeffrey Harrison is the author of *The Singing Underneath* and *Signs of Arrival.*

James Haug published a chapbook, *Foxluck*, with the Center for Book Arts, New York, and two collections, *The Stolen Car*, and *Walking Liberty*, which won the 1999 Morse Poetry Prize.

Robert Hayden's poetry was awarded two Hopwood Awards, the Grand Prize for Poetry at the First World Festival of Negro Arts, and the Russell Loines Award for distinguished poetic achievement from the National Institute of Arts and Letters. In 1975 he became a fellow of the Academy of American Poets and also served two terms as poetry consultant to the Library of Congress. He was professor of English at the University of Michigan and died in 1980 at the age of sixty-six.

David Hayward's poems have appeared in *ZYZZYVA*, the *Three Penny Review*, and other magazines.

William Heyen is professor of English and poet in residence at State University of New York at Brockport, his undergraduate alma mater, where he played basketball and was an All American in soccer. A former senior Fulbright lecturer in American literature in Germany, he has received NEA, Guggenheim, American Academy of Arts and Letters, and other fellowships. He is the editor of the anthologies *American Poets in 1976* and *The Generation of 2000: Contemporary American Poets.* His own books include *Depth of Field, Long Island Light, Erika: Poems of the Holocaust, Pterodactyl Rose: Poems of Ecology, Ribbons: The Gulf War, The Host: Selected Poems*, and *Crazy Horse in Stillness*, winner of 1997's Small Press Book Award for poetry. He has also published a memoir, *With Me Far Away*, and *Pig Notes & Dumb Music: Prose on Poetry.*

Frank Higgins is the author of a book of poems, *Starting from Ellis Island*, and a number of plays, including *The Sweet By 'n' By.*

Brenda Hillman is the author of five collections of poetry. She teaches at St. Mary's College in Moraga, California.

David Hilton has published several books of poetry, including *Huladance* and *No Reflection to the Hotel.* His poems have appeared in numerous literary journals, including *Poetry*, the *Iowa Review*, and the *Yale Review.* Since 1971 he has taught English at Anne Arundel Community College in Arnold, Maryland.

Edward Hirsch is the author of five books of poems and has received the National

Book Critics Circle Award, the Lavan Younger Poets Award from the Academy of American Poets, and the Delmore Schwartz Memorial Award from New York University. He has also received fellowships from the Guggenheim and MacArthur Foundations, an Ingram Merrill Foundation Award, a National Endowment for the Arts Fellowship, the Rome Prize from the American Academy in Rome, and a Lila Wallace–Reader's Digest Writers' Award. He teaches at the University of Houston.

Jonathan Holden is university distinguished professor of English, and poet-in-residence at Kansas State University. His most recent book is *Guns and Boyhood in America: A Memoir of Growing up in the 50s.*

Paul Hoover is the author of seven poetry collections, including *Totem and Shadow: New & Selected Poems, Viridian,* and *The Novel: A Poem.* He is also the editor of the anthology *Postmodern American Poetry* and the literary magazine *New American Writing.*

Richard Hugo was for many years the director of the creative writing program at the University of Montana, Missoula Campus. He received the Theodore Roethke Memorial Prize and was twice nominated for the National Book Award. He died in 1982.

David Ignatow is the author of eighteen volumes of poetry and three books of prose. In a career spanning more than fifty years, he received innumerable awards and fellowships. He was president emeritus of the Poetry Society of America from 1980 to 1984 and poet-in-residence at the Walt Whitman Birthplace Association in 1987, serving on its governing board in 1989. David Ignatow died at his home in East Hampton, New York, on November 17, 1997, at the age of eighty-three.

Mark Jarman's latest collection of poetry, *Question for Ecclesiates,* won the Lenore Marshall Poetry Prize in 1998 and was a finalist for the 1997 National Book Critics Circle Award. He is coeditor of *Rebel Angels: 25 Poets of New Formalism* and coauthor of *The Reaper Essays.* His books of essays *The Secret of Poetry* is forthcoming from Story Line Press, as is his next collection of poetry, *Unholy Sonnets.* He teaches at Vanderbilt University.

Randall Jarrell's collections include *Little Friend, Little Friend; Losses; The Woman at the Washington Zoo;* and *The Lost World.* He died in 1965 at the age of fifty.

Louis Jenkins lives in Duluth, Minnesota. His most recent book of poems is *Just above Water.* His prose poems were selected for inclusion in *The Best American Poetry,* 1999.

Galway Kinnell is a former MacArthur Fellow and has been state poet of Vermont. In 1982 his *Selected Poems* won the Pulitzer Prize and the National Book Award. He teaches at New York University, where he is the Erich Maria Remarque Professor of Creative Writing.

Carolyn Kizer has been poet-in-residence at many universities, including Columbia, Stanford, and Princeton. She served as the first Literature Program director at the National Endowment for the Arts. She was awarded the Pulitzer Prize for Poetry in 1985 and the Theodore Roethke Award in 1988. She lives in Sonoma, California.

August Kleinzahler's most recent collection of poems is *Green Sees Things in Waves*. He is the recipient of numerous awards, including a Guggenheim Fellowship, a Lila Wallace–Reader's Digest Writers' Award, and an award in literature from the American Academy of Arts and Letters. He lives in San Francisco.

Yusef Komunyakaa is professor of creative writing at Princeton University. He won the Pulitzer Prize and the Kingsley-Tufts Poetry Award for *Neon Vernacular*, one of his nine collections of poetry. *Thieves of Paradise*, his most recent collection, won the Morton Zabel Award from the American Academy of Arts and Letters.

Mark Kraushaar has received grants from the Wisconsin Arts Board. In 1991 he received Poetry Northwest's Richard Hugo Award. He works as an RN in Madison, Wisconsin.

Maxine Kumin has published eleven books of poetry, including *Up Country: Poems of New England*, for which she received the Pulitzer Prize. She is also the author of four novels, a collection of short stories, more than twenty children's books, and three books of essays, most recently, *Women, Animals, and Vegetables*. In addition to receiving several prestigious fellowships and prizes, she has served as consultant in poetry to the Library of Congress and poet laureate of New Hampshire and is a former chancellor of the Academy of American Poets. She lives in New Hampshire.

Tony Lacavaro's poems have appeared in the *Paris Review*, the *Western Humanities Review*, and the *Alembic* as well as *Ravishing Disunities: Real Ghazals in English*. He recently completed his first manuscript, "A Beautiful Nearby Suspect," and lives in Brooklyn, New York.

Adam Lefevre makes his living as an actor. A book of his poems, *Everything All at Once*, was published by Wesleyan University Press.

Philip Levine's most recent collection is *The Mercy*. His other most notable poetry collections include *The Simple Truth*, which won the Pulitzer Prize; *What Work Is*, which won the National Book Award; *Ashes: Poems New and Old*, which received the National Book Critics Circle Award and the first American Book Award for Poetry; *7 Years from Somewhere*, which won the National Book Critics Circle Award; and *The Names of the Lost*, which won the Lenore Marshall Poetry Prize. He has also published a collection of essays and coedited and translated two books. He is the recipient of numerous other fellowships and awards. For two years he served as chair of the Literature Panel of the National Endowment for the Arts. He lives in New York City and Fresno, California, and teaches at New York University.

Adrian Louis teaches at Southwest State University in Marshall, Minnesota. His most recent book of poems is *Ancient Acid Flashes Back*.

Thomas Lux's most recent collection is *New and Selected Poems 1975–1995*. He teaches at Sarah Lawrence College.

William Matthews, the author of a dozen books of poetry, won the National Book Critics Circle Award in 1995 for *Time & Money* and the Ruth Lilly Award of the Modern Poetry Association in 1997. He lives in New York.

James McKean has published two books of poetry *Headlong* and *Tree of Heaven*. He teaches at Mount Mercy College in Cedar Rapids, Iowa.

Christopher Merrill's books include *Watch Fire* (poetry), *Only the Nails Remain: Scenes from the Balkan Wars* (nonfiction), and translations of Ales Debeljak's *Anxious Moments* and *The City and the Child*.

Marianne Moore's *Collected Poems* won the Bollingen Prize, the National Book Award, and the Pulitzer Prize. She died in New York City, in her eighty-fifth year, on February 5, 1972.

Rick Noguchi's *The Ocean inside Kenji Takezo* won the 1995 Associated Writing Programs Award Series in poetry. His chapbook *The Wave He Caught* won the 1994 Pearl Editions Prize.

Lisa Olstein's poems have appeared in several literary journals.

Greg Pape is the author of several books, including *American Flamingo, Sunflower Facing the Sun*, and *A Storm Pattern*.

Linda Pastan's books include *Heroes in Disguise* and *An Early Afterlife*. *PM/AM* was a finalist for the National Book Award in 1982, and *The Imperfect Paradise* was a finalist for the Los Angeles Times Book Prize. Her most recent collection, *Carnival Evening: New and Selected Poems 1968–1998*, was a finalist for the National Book Award.

Marge Piercy is the author of fifteen novels, most recently *Three Women;* fourteen books of poetry, most recently *The Art of Blessing the Day: Poems with a Jewish Theme, Early Grrrl: The Early Poems of Marge Piercy*, and *What Are Big Girls Made Of?*

Stanley Plumly's *Out-of-the-Body Travel* won the William Carlos Williams Award and was nominated for the National Book Critics Circle Award. His *In the Outer Dark* won the Delmore Schwartz Memorial Award. His honors include a Guggenheim Fellowship, an Ingram-Merrill Foundation Fellowship, and a National Endowment for the Arts grant. He is a professor of English at the University of Maryland, College Park.

Jennifer Richter is a former Wallace Stegner Fellow and Jones Lecturer in Poetry at Stanford University. From 1995 to 1999 she served as poetry editor for *Sport Literate Magazine*. Her poems have appeared in *Poetry, Ploughshares, Puerto del Sol*, and other national journals.

David Roderick's poems and book reviews have appeared in several literary journals.

Theodore Roethke's *The Waking* was awarded the Pulitzer Prize in 1954. Theodore Roethke died in 1963.

Mary Jo Salter is the author of three previous collections of poems as well as a children's book. She is also an editor of *The Norton Anthology of Poetry*. An Emily Dickinson Lecturer in the humanities at Mount Holyoke College, she lives in South Hadley, Massachusetts, with her husband and their daughters.

Carl Sandburg was awarded the Pulitzer Prize for the second part of his Lincoln biography, *Abraham Lincoln: The War Years*, and a second Pulitzer Prize in 1950 for his *Complete Poems*. His final volumes of poetry were *Harvest Poems, 1910–1960* and *Honey and Salt*. He died in 1967.

Floyd Skloot's collections of poetry include *Music Appreciation* and *The Evening Light*. His poems have appeared in *Poetry*, the *Atlantic Monthly, Harper's*, the *Hudson Review*, the *Sewanee Review*, the *Southern Review*, and *Salmagundi*. He is also the author of three novels and a book of essays. He lives in Amity, Oregon.

Dave Smith's most recent book of poems is *The Wick of Memory: New and Selected Poems 1970–2000*. He is Boyd Professor of English at Louisiana State University and coeditor of the *Southern Review*.

R. T. Smith's books include *Trespasser, Split the Lark*, and *Messenger*. He lives in Rockbridge County, Virginia, and is editor of *Shenandoah*.

Alan Soldofsky directs the Creative Writing Program at San Jose State University. He has published two chapbooks of poems, *Kenora Station* and *Staying Home*.

Gary Soto is the author of ten poetry collections, most notably *New and Selected Poems*, a 1995 finalist for both the Los Angeles Times Book Award and the National Book Award. His recollections, *Living up the Street*, received a Before Columbus Foundation 1985 American Book Award. He edits the Chicano Chapbook series and is distinguished professor of creative writing at the University of California at Riverside.

David St. John's most recent collections are *The Red Leaves of Night* and *In the Pines: Lost Poems, 1972–1997*.

William Stafford is the author of more than fifty books and recipient of the National Book Award for *Traveling through the Dark*. He was a professor at Lewis & Clark College, served as consultant in poetry to the Library of Congress in 1970, and was named Oregon's poet laureate in 1975. He was born in Hutchinson, Kansas, in 1914 and died in Oregon in 1993.

Martín Steingesser's poems have appeared in the *American Poetry Review*, the *Beloit Poetry Journal*, the *Progressive*, and the op-ed page of the *New York Times*. His story *The Wildman*, with blockprints by Vermont artist Mary Azarian, is published by North Country Press. He would like to find a publisher for his poetry manuscript.

Dabney Stuart has published twelve previous volumes of poetry, including *Long Gone* and *Light Years: New and Selected Poems*. He is professor of English at Washington and Lee University in Lexington, Virginia.

James Tate's most recent volume of poems is *Shroud of the Gnome*.

Quincy Troupe is a featured poet on Bill Moyers's PBS series *The Power of the Word* and is the author of *Miles & Me*. He is the coauthor of the bestseller *Miles: The Autobiography* and the editor of *James Baldwin: The Legacy*. The winner of two American Book Awards, Troupe teaches at the University of California at San Diego. His most recent book of poetry is *Choruses*.

Dennis Trudell's *Fragments in Us: Recent and Earlier Poems* won the 1996 Pollack Prize from the University of Wisconsin Press. He is editor of *Full Court: A Literary Anthology of Basketball*. Trudell's poems and short stories have appeared in many literary journals. A basketball story, "Gook," was selected for a recent O. Henry Prize.

Ron Wellburn's poems have appeared in over one hundred literary magazines and anthologies, including *Gatherings: The En'owkin Journal of First North American*

Peoples, The Phoenix, Returning the Gift, Callaloo, and *Best American Poetry, 1997.* His sixth collection of poems, *Coming through Smoke and the Dreaming,* will be published by Greenfield Review Press. He teaches in the English Department at the University of Massachusetts at Amherst and is director of the Native American Indian Studies Program. He is an Assateague Cherokee and of African American descent.

Richard Wilbur's most recent book of poetry is his *New and Collected Poems* which won the Pulitzer Prize. He was elected a chevalier of the Ordre des Palmes Académiques and is a former poet laureate of the United States. A chancellor emeritus of the Academy of American Poets, he lives in Cummington, Massachusetts.

William Carlos Williams's major poetry works include *Kora in Hell, Spring and All, Pictures from Brueghel and Other Poems,* for which he won a Pulitzer Prize, the five-volume epic *Paterson,* and *Imaginations.* He continued writing until his death in New Jersey in 1963.

James Wright was elected a fellow of the Academy of American Poets in 1971, and a year later his collected poems, *Above the River,* received the Pulitzer Prize in Poetry. He died in New York in 1980.

Acknowledgments

Thank you, David Roderick, Daniel Mahoney, and Kendra Borgmann for your
editorial assistance. Additional thanks to Agha Shahíd Ali, Martín Espada,
Herman Fong, Forrest Hamer, Pierce Johnston, Priscilla Lee, Dave Morris,
Kevin Pruffer, and Christopher Merrill, who, as my grandfather would say,
has been a mensch. Gratitude to Stephen Clingman.

Diane Ackerman: "Pumping Iron," from *Jaguar of Sweet Laughter: New & Selected
Poems* (Random House, 1991). Copyright © 1991 by Diane Ackerman. Reprinted
by permission of the author.

Kim Addonizio: "Event" and "Late Round," from *The Philosopher's Club* (BOA
Editions, 1994). Copyright © 1994 by Kim Addonizio. Reprinted by permission
of the author.

Elizabeth Alexander: "Narrative: Ali," first published in *Every Shut Eye Ain't
Asleep*, edited by Michael S. Harper and Anthony Walton (Little, Brown, 1994).
Copyright © 1994 by Elizabeth Alexander. Used by permission of the author.

Sherman Alexie: "Penance," from *The Business of Fancydancing* (Hanging Loose
Press, 1992), and "Why We Play Basketball," from *The Summer of Black Widows*
(Hanging Loose Press, 1996). Copyright © 1992, 1996 by Sherman Alexie.
Reprinted by permission of Hanging Loose Press.

Agha Shahid Ali: "The Jogger on Riverside Drive, 5:00 A.M.," from *The Half-Inch
Himalayas* (Wesleyan University Press, 1987). Copyright © 1987 by Agha Shahid
Ali. Reprinted by permission of University Press of New England.

Sam Allen: "To Satch." Reprinted by permission of the author.

Craig Arnold: "Locker Room Etiquette," from *Shells* (Yale University Press, 1999).
Copyright © 1999 by Craig Arnold. Reprinted by permission of Yale University
Press.

George Barlow: "A Dream of the Ring: The Great Jack Johnson," from *Soledad*.
Copyright © 1994 by George Barlow. Reprinted by permission of the author.

Dorothy Barresi: "Called Up: Tinker to Evers to Chance," from *The Post Rapture
Diner* (Beacon Press, 1991). Copyright © 1991 by Dorothy Barresi. Reprinted
by permission of the author. "Lifting," from *All of the Above* (University of
Pittsburgh Press, 1996). Copyright © 1996 by Dorothy Barresi. Reprinted
by permission of the author.

Norman Dubie: "The Death of the Race Car Driver," from *Groom Falconer* (W. W. Norton, 1989). Copyright © by Norman Dubie. Reprinted by permission of the author.

Stephen Dunn: "Competition" and "Day and Night Handball" were published in *New & Selected Poems: 1974–1994*. Copyright © 1994 by Stephen Dunn. "Criminal" was published in *Loosefire*. Copyright © 1996 by Stephen Dunn. Used by permission of W. W. Norton and Company, Inc.

Cornelius Eady: "Jack Johnson Does the Eagle Rock." Reprinted by permission of the author.

Jon Engels: "Bullhead," from *Big Water* (Lyons Press, 1994). Reprinted by permission of the author.

Martín Espada: "The Man Who Beat Hemingway," from *Imagine the Angels of Bread*. Copyright © 1996 by Martín Espada. Reprinted by permission of W. W. Norton & Company, Inc.

David Allan Evans: "Pole Vaulter" was first published in *Esquire* (November 1972). "Song of Racquetball" was first published in *Shenandoah* 40, no. 3 (Fall 1990). Reprinted by permission of the author.

B. H. Fairchild: "Body and Soul" and "Old Men Playing Basketball," from *The Art of the Lathe* (Alice James Books, 1998). Copyright © by B. H. Fairchild.

Lawrence Ferlinghetti: "Baseball Canto," from *These Are My Rivers*. Copyright © 1993 by Lawrence Ferlinghetti. Reprinted by permission of New Directions Publishing Corp.

Gary Fincke: "Class A, Salem, the Rookie League" originally appeared in the *Gettysburg Review;* collected in *Blood Ties* (Time Being Books, 2001). Reprinted by permission of the author.

Robert Francis: "Pitcher," "The Rock Climbers," and "Two Wrestlers," from *Orb Weaver* (Wesleyan University Press, 1960). Copyright © 1960 by Robert Francis. Reprinted by permission of University Press of New England.

Carol Frost: "Custom," from *Venus and Don Juan* (Northwestern University Press, 1996). First published in the *Southern Review*. "To Kill a Deer" from *Pure* (Northwestern University Press, 1994). First published in the *Missouri Review*.

Brendan Galvin: "The Knot Hole Gang," from *Seals in the Inner Harbor*. Reprinted by permission of Carnegie Mellon University Press. Copyright © 1986 by Brendan Galvin. "Running," from *Great Blue: New and Selected Poems*. Copyright © 1990 by Brendan Galvin. Reprinted by permission of the author and the University of Illinois Press.

Index